Eyes Guided by God

A MEMOIR

Janvier F. Nsengiyumva

Burlington, Vermont

Onion River Press
191 Bank Street
Burlington, VT 05401
info@onionriverpress.com
www.onionriverpress.com

ISBN: 978-1-957184-20-3

Contents

EYES GUIDED BY GOD

1

Introduction

I was born in a refugee camp in Tanzania in 1997. My parents crossed paths with two of the most horrific genocides of the 20th century, first in Burundi and next in Rwanda. The two mass killings are linked by history, culture, and memories of deeply embedded enmity between Hutus and Tutsis. The first "Great Calamity," the Burundian *Ikiza*, erupted in 1972 when Tutsis slaughtered Hutus and 300,000 died and hundreds of thousands lost their homes. At that time, my parents fled from Burundi into their northern neighbor, Rwanda. There they lived peacefully until the second "Scourge" of the Rwandan Genocide exploded in 1994 when Hutus slaughtered Tutsis and 800,000 died.

I did not witness these catastrophes. Instead, I spent my babyhood watching our neighbors pass by our house in the refugee camp. As I have grown older, I have learned about the Great Calamity and the Rwandan Genocide by reading, googling, watching movies, and listening to my parents' own words and watching their eyes. Together, the movies, *Sometimes in April* and *Rwanda Hotel*, do capture a sense of nightmare, but perhaps only people whose lives have been shocked overnight from their quiet lives into a world of outrageous violence and death, people like Bosnians or Syrians or Ukrainians and my parents, can truly comprehend the horror.

As I listen to my parents reminisce about their peaceful lives in Rwanda, I hear the sublime music of a soft guitar, music that touches sweet nostalgia in their hearts. They remember the rhythm of their days, sharing music and laughter; sharing the work–my father tailoring clothes, my mother raising crops; sharing the children they created, cared for, and loved. These memories nestle in my heart; the hard times since then tear at my heart.

 Situated near the equator, Burundi and Rwanda are small countries nestled together in the lake region of eastern Africa. To the west lies the much larger Democratic Republic of the Congo and to the east and south is Tanzania, a place of refuge for many escaping ethnic violence. Uganda lies to the north.

Burundi and Rwanda are closely related in size, population, language, culture, and history. Most people speak the Bantu languages of Ki-

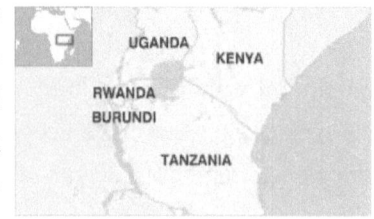

rundi in Burundi and Kinyarwanda in Rwanda. French, the language of the Belgian colonizers, is spoken by an educated elite although it has been absorbed more broadly in a mixed vernacular of the native language. Swahili is also spoken as the language of trade and communication with East African neighbors. English has recently been introduced in Rwanda.

The three ethnic groups in both countries are Hutu, Tutsi, and the pygmy forest dwellers, Twa. The inherently minor differences between the Hutus and Tutsi were exacerbated during the nineteenth and twentieth centuries by the European colonialists, who set the lighter-skinned Tutsis who owned cattle above the more numerous, darker-skinned Hutus who were farmers in the power structure. As a result, tensions between the two groups have long festered and, too often, burst into horrific violence.

Thus, when the Burundian *Ikiza* occurred, my parents naturally sought refuge in Rwanda where much was familiar to them. There they built a happy life together. They lived in a comfortable house on a small farm, located near the city of Nyagatare. My father designed and sewed colorful dresses and wrapped skirts to be sold in the village bazaar. My mother would rise at dawn to tend the ducks, tomatoes, beans, and corn. She would cook meals and care for the children. They were happy and content with the work, children, and music that enriched their lives. This is the home my mother still dreams of and yearns for.

The bloody Rwandan Genocide started quickly. My father remembers that "no one anticipated anything." On April 7, 1994, the sounds of gunshots filled the air. Hutus across

Rwanda were murdering Tutsis with rifles and machetes. Families began to flee from this frenzy of killing through the forests and jungles. In the turmoil, many families were scattered; some children were even left behind. My parents had little time to grab sleeping blankets and bundles of food. They could hear the sound of shotguns moving closer; it was a matter of life and death. They ran with their children into the woods. My mother carried the baby, Desta, slung on her back. She carried a sack bag on her head. The four girls, Bebe, Tina, Niyo, and Fana, were holding hands and walking beside my mother. My father followed them, pushing a bicycle with the oldest boy, Ife, sitting on it.

Several families banded together for the long trek east to the border separating Rwanda and Tanzania and then southward along the Kagera (Akagera River) River. My parents and others were familiar with this kind of desperate journey; Many of them had escaped from Burundi in 1972, and now, once again, they were headed into an unknown future.

Walking more than 100 miles through savannas and cypress swamps, their bare feet were cracked and bleeding until the callouses hardened them. At first, crossing the fields outside of Nyagatera and the open savannahs, the band of exiles crowded together for safety, but so tightly were they packed that each person had to wait for the person ahead to take a step before they could follow. It seemed like a giant tortoise shuffling slowly along the path. When they reached the relative safety of the woodlands, people could spread out, breathe more deeply, and move more quickly.

With the Kagera River as their guide, they headed south, back towards Burundi. Thousands of slaughtered corpses were being dumped into the river, clogging the flow all the way to Lake Victoria in the north. Gunshots rang out day and night. Desperate souls, with gunshot and machete wounds, staggered by. Many died along the way. The group would pause to bury each one, marking the grave with a simple cross made of wood. It was a fearful diaspora.

Passing through the marshes and cypress swamps of the Akagera National Park, my parents shepherded the family along. Exhausted, hungry, and always alert, my mother and father kept walking with their six children. When the children cried, "We are hungry," my mother would pause to hug them and sigh, "We will find something. God will guide us." They drank water from the river and ate fruit ripening on trees. Some people even ate the mud left by the rain. At night, some of the exiles kept walking; others pitched tents to keep dry and warm while they rested. My parents did not have a tent, so the family slept on the ground. But even as they journeyed, they welcomed another child, my older sister, Ajani.

Thankfully, Tanzania welcomed hundreds of thousands refugees from the civil wars of Burundi and Rwanda during this time. When our own band of Burundian families finally arrived at the refugee camp near Ngara in Tanzania, just south of Lake Rweru, they at last found safety, food, and a place to rest. The arriving refugees were provided with strong, waterproof poly tarps for shelter and food from the United Nations High Commissioner for Refugees (UNHCR) and the

United Nations Children's Emergency Fund (UNICEF). The camp became my family's home.

2

The Refugee Camp

The refugee camp in Tanzania was isolated where our existence seemed limited. In the distance, I could see a large jungle that would give me the illusion that the world ended by passing the tropical trees, plants, and swamps. My family would travel to the jungle to collect wood for the cooking fire built on stones. I was too young to go with them into the jungle.

The refugee camp was not a place to stay forever. It was a camp for people without a country.

The days were hot and humid except for the rainy season in the springtime called *uru-shāna*. It would rain hard, particularly in April. The pouring rain caused mud. Sometimes people would accidentally slip in the mud. It was comforting to sleep at night when it rained; the sound of raindrops falling on the roof relaxed me.

During the heat of the day, the surface ground would

conduct heat from the sun and cause your bare feet to burn even though people learned to get used to it. Sometimes while playing in the yard, I would feel my feet burning.

As a little boy, the only three things in the world I knew were the mud, the food we ate every morning and night, and the jungle from a distance—too dangerous for  a young boy. The jungle was described by people in the camp as " beautiful" because of the acacia and eucalyptus trees, the flowing water, the swamps where kids would swim, the birds, and all kinds of fruits like mango, bananas, and pineapples. Desta described it as "the Garden of Eve" particularly because Tanzania is the place where humans emerged.

 Called Rukore, the refugee camp was built on a grid with numbered streets, not on barren ground but a savannah with fever trees throughout, breaking the monotony. The houses were constructed with wood from nearby trees and mud bricks baked in the sun. The wooden support beams seemed slender and shaky. The roofs were sturdier, made of wood with banana leaves and blue tarps spread over them. Most of the houses had the front door facing away from the street and leading into the yards behind the houses.

My family lived on 39 Street. Our house was larger than

most, but uglier, I felt. I really don't know why; perhaps because when the upper, layered, blue tarp covering the roof would flap in the wind and fold back, the house seemed especially uglier and misshapen. Our house was built with mud bricks and had a porch made of sticks and mud where we could sit outside and feel the cooling breezes. During the evening, after we ate, my family would sit outside on the ground in front of the house and tell each other stories or share the latest rumors. As my siblings talked, I would gaze up at the sky and try to make sense of the constellations.

The camp was a small community of refugees mostly from Burundi; a community for people who shared a common consciousness of culture, tradition, and of violence. They also shared a faith and trust in both

Christianity and the traditional belief of an all pervasive life force. Roman Catholicism arrived in Burundi and Rwanda with the German and Belgian priests in the nineteenth- and twentieth-centuries, and the refugee camp's church with its European priest was supported and attended by nearly all the residents.

Storytelling is traditional in Burundian culture. Families would gather together in the camp to tell these ancient stories, passing them down through the generations. The men would tell the stories as  they whispered, singing and playing the *inanga*, an eight-stringed instrument with a flat soundboard. A man in traditional attire of a bright patterned robe playing an inanga carved from wood might whisper as he tells a story, interweaving the narrative by singing:

> Ndamubabaye: I am sorry,
> Ndamubabaye: I am sorry,
> Ndamubabaye: I am sorry,
> Ndamubabaye: I am sorry,
> Nkunda amahoro, mu Burundi bwacu: I love peace in
>   our country Burundi.

And Burundians love to sing. The families who lived in the camp sang songs of yearning and hope, but mostly they sang about loss. The songs expressed trust in the loving, Christian God. Belief in this God held the camp together. I heard these songs every day growing up in church while singing from hymnals and while listening to my siblings singing as we sat together at home on the porch. They were sorrowful songs that touched the hearts of the people in the camp. There was a longing to escape the reality of our situation. For some, angels were coming down to carry us home as in the spiritual, "Swing Low, Sweet Chariot":

> Swing low, sweet chariot
> Coming for to carry me home
> Swing low, sweet chariot
> Coming for to carry me home
>
> I looked over Jordan, and what did I see
> Coming for to carry me home

A band of angels coming after me
Coming for to carry me home

Swing low, sweet chariot
Coming for to carry me home
Swing low, sweet chariot
Coming for to carry me home

If you get there before I do
Coming for to carry me home
Tell all my friends I'm coming, too
Coming for to carry me home

Other songs were our own; one in Kirundi that I remember:

> Guhunga Kwabo mwisi
> Bageze Muri Canada,
> Tuzababona gute?
> Abaturanyi bacu
> Bageze muri Tanzania,
> Tuzababona gute?
> Abaturanyi bacu
> Uyu mugabo bavuga ni Yesu,
> Ubuhungiro bwimpunzi
> Yesu ni ubuhungiro bwabantu
>
> People fleeing on earth.
> They fled to Canada,
> How are we going to see them?

Our neighbors, how are we going to see them?
They fled to Tanzania,
This man they talk about is Jesus,
His is the refuge of the refugees.
Jesus is the refuge of the people.

This song helped assuage the pain and grief and suffering of the Burundian refugees. In these songs, the people would remember being uprooted from their homes and forced to flee because of the terrible violence of the genocides in Burundi and in Rwanda. In the songs, the people grieve for the ones who died as they ran, and lament that, as we flew in all directions, we would never be home again; we would never be reconciled with our people until, at last, we reached heaven.

Although life seemed peaceful in the camp at first, the longer we lived in the camp, the more tensions bubbled up. Ethnic rivalries emerged. Not everyone was purely Burundian or Rwandan. Not everyone was purely Tutsi or Hutu. Families were mixed and frictions sparked old and new angers and mistrust. Gangs were formed, theft became more common, and even murders took place. Life in the camp was becoming more violent. Often at night, you would hear shotguns blasting. I was asleep when I first heard a gunshot, but I instantly knew what it was; I held tightly to my sheet while curling up my legs, making myself as tiny and invisible as possible.

While there were political and ethnic tensions, money was often the force driving the violence. If it became known that you were making money or were rich, you were a target for these thieves. They would break into your house at night, kill you in your sleep, and take all your money. I heard that one man was stabbed to death in front of his children. Such news was heartbreaking and haunting. I put my head down my chest as my heart jumped in fear, saying to myself, I am glad we are not rich.

Desta came home one time and told my mother that a boy had been shot last night while peeing outside. The guns would blast throughout the night, keeping us awake. And now an innocent boy's life had been brutally taken. I overheard my sister Niyo saying that these thieves were people we knew who lived in the neighborhood. "They walk through the neighborhood during the day; we talk to them; they are our friends," she said. With no police protection, the adults organized a neighborhood watch. This group, mostly men from the neighborhood, were responsible for keeping the area safe. Unfortunately, even the neighborhood watch couldn't stop all the violence. I heard that occasionally the Tanzanian police were called, but I never saw anyone in a police uniform.

After the news about the boy who was killed while peeing at night, kids like me were always cautious. We had to deal with this strange peril of our condition. For the most part, I was terrified to go outside at night to pee because it was so dark. If the moon did not appear, I could barely see where I was peeing. We each had an outhouse by our house, but it did not feel safe, especially at night since there were no lights. When I had to go at night, I would feel my heart beating with fear that oppressed my mind. Any rustling of the wind would make me panic. If I heard even the slightest sound, I would run quickly into the house. Sometimes I didn't even finish peeing, so I had to take the chance of peeing on myself.

3

Memories of a
Little Boy

I was the first child my parents gave birth to in the camp. From the moment I was born, the sun was on my face. My sense of time came from watching the sun and shadows cross the sky and land. When the sun was high above, it was hot and halfway through the day. Or it rained and rained and everywhere was mud. I knew nothing of months or years as they passed. There were simply two seasons: dry and wet. I was simply a boy living in my playground of dirt or mud and had little perception of time passing.

Most of the time, the world around me was too busy with surviving to even notice me. I particularly remember one of those days when I was about five years old. It was a hot day, and the sun was burning my face and sweat was dripping from my forehead. I was out in the neighborhood looking for pieces of wood for my playhouse. In my favorite clothes—brown shorts and a soft but tattered brown t-shirt—I had no fear of getting dirty.

My timidity could be seen on my face and my eyes would glimmer latent melancholy. My lips were always dry, and I still had leftover food smeared on the corner of my mouth. My mother cut my hair short; it was cooler that way and easier to wash. My sister would tease me that my face was lopsided—my right cheek was chubbier than my left cheek because I always slept on the left side. My two younger sisters and I were still children, so we slept on the same bed with our mother and father. It was a hard bed without a mattress, made with brick and mud, but we had blankets for warmth and softness. I slept below my parents, lying across their feet. My sisters would sleep next to them.

When I was about two- or three-years-old, I became ill with a long-lasting form of malaria which plagued me for years. One long-term effect of the disease was that I was anemic, small, and, at times, unable to hold down my food. I thought I was becoming a skeleton—so I chose solitary games rather than the rough and tumble sport of other kids.

Even in the hubbub of a large family, my mother would try to make sure I ate. I tended to lose myself building a mud house and not thinking about eating, so often I would arrive late for dinner. I remember one time coming into the kitchen after everyone had eaten dinner. I was so hungry by then that I lifted the lid on the dutch oven and looked inside to see if there was any leftover food, but I found only a small piece of corn *fufu*. One piece of corn *fufu* was not enough to relieve my hunger. I complained to my mother, asking her why they didn't leave enough food for me.

I grew up sitting at home, watching a world whose purpose I couldn't quite grasp. The other kids seemed strange to me; I couldn't engage in their everyday games. One time, I was walking across the street to find friends. Two unfamiliar boys walked up to me and started laughing at me, pushing me on my shoulder, and calling me names. "It's the skinny boy with uneven cheeks," one of the boys said while others heckled. And so, unlike the other children, I preferred to stay at home, building my own playhouse.

Whenever I heard the rooster crow, I would wake early in the morning to pee outside my house near the rainwater flowing down the muddy hill slope. I would feel the breeze as I watched the bright sunrise shining against the buildings. I would stare at the long shadows of the trees and houses while continuing to breathe the morning cool air. But the morning breeze would never last; it would ebb away as the sun moved up high, heating up the world and causing me to sweat from my forehead. The shed was the safest place to sit and enjoy the day. People in the camp sat outside of their houses in the shade of their sheds to avoid the sweltering heat.

There was a field of dirt nearby, where I watched boys in bare feet playing soccer. Other boys in the street were riding handmade wooden bicycles or playing with handmade wire toy cars that had a long wire that pushed the car on one end guided by a steering wheel on the other end. There were other kids playing a game called *akamarimari*; using a stick with a rope tied to the end, the boys would whip a small wooden cone to keep it spinning like a top. I never played the game, but it was fun watching others enjoying it.

During the day while sitting in my playground, I would listen to the sounds of the wind blowing through the leaves of the trees, pigeons cooing, and birds fluttering their wings. I felt, rather than heard, the sounds of people in the camp; the feelings were of a yearning, a straining, for life in an unsettled, and too often violent, refuge. I would hear babies crying. I would watch as babies were wrapped in brightly colored shawls on their mothers' backs; whenever a baby fussed, the mother would reach back and gently pat the baby's bottom. I would hear kids running on the street, girls singing rhymes as they swung jump ropes back and forth, and I could also hear distant laughter and what seemed to be a hurrying world that would cease to calm down, relax, or feel truly safe.

As I sat there in the yard under the shed, in the late afternoon, I would observe the world around me. I would count how many people were walking by my house. Some were talking, laughing, and others were in a hurry. I would watch my sister Niyo and other girls next door standing in the middle of the street and talking. I thought they were perhaps engaging in their usual gossip from the way they laughed, giggling about someone.

I would also notice that during the day when the sun was still shining and cooking smoke was blowing from every neighbors' kitchen, the fathers were often absent from their homes. I would only see mothers or daughters sitting in the kitchen cooking or cleaning the yard. The daughters would be learning the tasks assigned to the women: first and most importantly, being present at home and then sweeping the yard, washing clothes, and cooking. As they grew, the sons who followed in the footsteps of their fathers also disappeared from home. Many fathers would go to the river to fish. Others, like my father, went to work each day.

At the intersection one block from my house, there was a water point, a faucet where we could collect clean water. Each morning, young women like my older sisters, wearing the colorful, traditional wrap skirts and headscarves, would come with water containers on their heads and queue up in a long line to fill their vessels with water for the day. Here they would greet friends and share news and gossip. After filling the containers, the women would place them back on their heads and walk carefully home.

Often the water faucet was broken, leaving all of us without water to drink or cook with. When there was no water, I remember my throat becoming so dry that I could barely swallow and my head would begin to throb. Those throbbing headaches are pounded into my memory.

As a little boy, it was difficult to understand who the people were who lived in the neighborhood. I was aware that they got along with each other for the most part. However, as I continued to observe people closely, I learned that sometimes there were certain people you might not like based on their behavior. For example, there was a woman next door who had a reputation for being rude. I used to watch her argue with another neighbor across from her. My sisters didn't say nice things about her, perhaps because of the harsh looks she wore on her face. She did not appear to be a likable person, and this was the case for neighbors who had bad reputations. She was short with a heavy body that made her look slightly overweight, and whenever her eyes landed on me, I felt that she was criticizing me.

I was terrified of this heavy woman because of her strident voice. Often, she would call her son's name so loudly that it echoed from a distance, "Rugamba Rugamba! Where are you?" she would cry in her Kinyarwanda accent. Suspicions about her later forced her and her son to return to Rwanda.

Rugamba, her son, was about my age and looked more like his father whom I rarely ever saw. Rugamba had a lean face and narrow shoulders. He was a well-mannered boy, but I could see the same loneliness in his eyes that I felt on my own. He had a gentle heart that deeply touched my heart. Sometimes the rude woman would shout his name while we were playing in the yard. I saw the fear in Rugamba, his body shook when he heard his mother calling him. Rugamba was his parents' only child, so his mother would force him to do the chores and clean the house, girl's work. I didn't have to do any of that since I had so many older sisters. I felt sorry for Rugamba, and watching him clean the yard alone made me want to help.

Our neighbors across from us were more pleasant than Rugamba's mother. The parents had four daughters who socialized with my sisters. The youngest daughter, Selina, was deaf; she would often come to my house looking for my little sisters. One day we were eating dinner as

a family from the communal platters. I was sitting down in the living room facing my siblings and with two platters in front of me. One had a large piece of corn *fufu*, and the other was filled with soup and small silver fish or sardines from Lake Tanganyika called *indagara* in Kirundi. Each of us would pull off pieces of *fufu* with our washed hands and dip the *fufu* into the soup, scooping up the fish. As we ate, I could see Selina standing outside, I looked at her with uncomfortable anger in my heart. I did not want another person to join us because there wouldn't be enough for me to eat.

Next to their home, these neighbors had a small square-shaped house built out of mud and wood like some of the houses. Inside, there were chairs and tables where adults like my father would go to drink a kind of beer called *urwagwa*. It is made with the juice of smashed bananas distilled in wooden casks. The men would drink *urwagwa* from a round vessel with a slender neck called *agacuma*. My father used to meet friends at this bar and come home drunk, and I remember watching him one night talking to another father who lived across the street from us. Their conversation felt distant, so I didn't get to hear every word, but I heard my father saying something sharply in French "*Mon Dieu, mon Dieu.*" I think he was upset, reacting to something.

When my father was at home, he always turned on his FM radio to listen to the news. He would turn up the volume so loud, it woke me up every morning. The sound of dialing sounded like a broken signal; "Shhhhh Shhhh" *Urakoze* (thank you) Shhhh". My father would move the antenna around to get a better reception. I listened with my father to news about Burundi and Rwanda; newscasters would speak in Kinyarwanda or Kirundi, but it didn't matter because I understood the gist of the messages. In this way, I learned about Burundi and Rwanda. Everything I heard about Burundi made me want to love Rwanda more. Sometimes a newscaster would say, "*intambara mu burundi*" translated as "war in Burundi'." From 1993 to 2005, Burundi was again engaged in, and suffering from, civil war. At that time around 2003, I heard nothing negative about Rwanda, so I desperately wanted my family to go to Rwanda instead of Burundi. I did not yet know that we were refugees from both countries, and neither one was an option for us to settle.

The neighbors next door on our right were middle-aged parents who were raising a young girl close to my age. Her name was Fayi. I didn't talk to her because she made me nervous. She seemed strange to me. I would glance at her squatting to pee in front of the small outhouse next to her house. It was normal for small children to pee outside instead of going into the outhouse because the outhouses were sometimes unsafe, especially early in the morning and night; you never knew who was hiding in it. What bothered me about Fayi was that we would wake up in the morning and pee at the same time. Every time I was peeing outside, I would look up and see her squatting doing the same thing. It was awkward, but it also frustrated me. I would try to avoid looking at her.

Fayi and I were about the same age, she was a little older. I would see her at school sitting alone, away from other girls who were jumping rope. I made eye contact with her for a second during recess and immediately looked down in shyness. I would stand forlornly with my hands in my pocket while nervously watching other other kids play. My mother would always tell me to go to school with her, but I would refuse because I felt so shy.

4

My Family

My mother is called Uwera. In those days in the refugee camps, she was in her early 40s. She worried especially about me as I struggled for so long with the after-effects of malaria. But she took care of all of us.

I remember my mother then as a woman with a thin face and slim body. She had the wise eyes of experience. I had never seen her hair because her head was always wrapped with a blue and red scarf. She wore the traditional eastern African fabric called *kitenge*, a vibrantly colorful patterned fabric that all women in the town wore. My mother was calm and kind. She was a Christian; I used to listen to her sing Christian songs while cooking in the kitchen. Her voice would bring me to tears, it touched deep in my heart. She was affectionate as a mother who loved her children dearly.

She would walk twenty minutes every morning to the UNICEF food distribution tents which were secured behind chain-link fences. I would often go with her and we would stand in line to receive our family's share of dried beans, corn kernels, or even ground corn in white sack bags. Whenever my mother received corn kernels, we would go to the corn mill near our house to have the kernels ground into corn-meal. The machine was so loud that it shook the ground. Then we would return home, so she could begin to grind the dried corn into cornmeal and cook the corn fufu for the day.

Sometimes I would go with my mother to fetch the food. Street kids were always present inside and outside the chain-link fence, scratching for leftover kernels of corn or beans. They would be sitting on their feet with their eyes on the ground, picking up dried beans that people dropped on the floor and stowing them in their pockets or in a jar. A few of them would try to steal from anyone, the people waiting in line, those leaving with their allotment, or even from another street kid, but then those foolish thieves would be caught by the police who were always present there.

I used to watch her cook in the kitchen, putting wood on the stove, lighting the fire, blowing on it to catch and burn the wood, with the smoke spreading out through the kitchen. The smoke was a sure sign that the food was being cooked. When I was hungry, with my stomach rumbling, I would wait when my mother was out of the kitchen. Then I would slowly walk in, and dip my hand in the dutch oven for the yellow peas that were still being cooked. Sometimes, though, as I was trying to eat them, my mother would come in and hit my hand and make me drop the peas. She hated it when someone touched the food before it was ready to be served. She would say to the thief, "This makes you a bad child."

I was very close to my mother, but sometimes I felt ignored because her attention was often taken up by my older sisters who were constantly fighting. With my father often absent, my mother had to deal with all the children. Being the youngest boy meant that I was often overlooked because I didn't cause problems or cry like my sisters. But, despite being the youngest boy among sisters, I may have been ignored at times, but I didn't feel neglected by my mother; she was always there for me, making sure I ate or took a shower. Since I was only six years old, it was normal to shower outside. She would bathe me and rinse me after rubbing me with soap. The fresh air dried my skin.

My father is called Izaak. He had been a tailor in Rwanda and continued to make clothes once in the refugee camp. He would go out of the camp to the marketplace of Ngara where he had his own market stall where he would hang up the clothes he was selling, and there would be customers gathered around checking out the style and fabric. He sold his pre-made clothes, and he also took orders from customers for bespoke clothes.

On Saturdays, the marketplace was especially busy, with people buying, selling, and eating. There were small market stalls with the products displayed or fruit and vegetable carts shaded by umbrellas. Bananas, rice, sweet potatoes, beans, sugar, and wheat flour were always available, and in season, one could buy fruits such as mangoes, oranges, papaya, pineapple and vegetables–carrots, eggplant, peppers, and spinach. When I went there with my mother, I saw people on bikes carrying green bananas on the back of their bike seats, and men crossing the road, bent over with molded plastic containers of soda. I watched women who were gaily dressed like my mother carrying baskets of rosy, golden mangoes. The market was full of colors, sounds, and life.

In the market, I could hear music from Lucky Dube playing in the distance. Lucky Dube was a South African reggae musician who was a Dub artist, a musical platform for the expression of displacement from the homeland. I remember hearing songs like "Back to My Roots," "Remember Me," and "Mama." Lucky Dube's songs were so popular on the radio that you could hear them anywhere you went, particularly in busy places like the market or even on a sunny afternoon sitting in front of the house.

As a child, I was not as close to my father as to my mother. When he was at home, he would work at his sewing machine. He never looked up to speak to me; his eyes focused on the presser foot of the machine, the handwheel, and pedal foot. He would make my mother's

clothes and other dresses to sell in the marketplace. He had a black battery-operated radio with a silver antenna sitting on his sewing machine so that he could listen to Burundian news. He carried the radio wherever he went. I would watch him carefully walking, limping slightly, and playing music or news on his radio. I always wondered why he walked like he was limping his right leg. I didn't know him well enough to even greet him. When he was home, he barely spoke. He would come home late in the afternoon, glance quickly at me, and walk inside the house to sleep after a long day. Every morning, he would put on his tie to go to work, and later, he would arrive at home with money in his pocket for my mother to buy clothes for us and food to eat.

My father had a big stomach, a brown skin complexion, and a full stubble beard that distinguished him in the town. His face was serious all the time. Because of his stubbly beard, neighbors thought he looked like the American martial arts and movie star Chuck Norris, who was very popular in the camp. Once when I was playing in the yard outside of the house, digging holes in the ground, it was almost evening. I looked up and saw my father heading home. As he was opening the wooden door, a tall, balding man standing on the street stopped him and said: "Hey, Chuck Norris!" I didn't know if it was an insult or a compliment; I didn't know who Chuck Norris was. But my father looked at him, waved his hand, and smiled, so he must have accepted it as a compliment.

My mother cooked in the small kitchen that was attached to the house. Only one person could fit in it. We ate twice a day. In the morning we would have a typical breakfast drink called *igikoma,* a nutritious meal made with quinoa flour. Sometimes it was so hot, my tongue burned when I tried to drink quickly. I would start blow on it to chase off the hotness. In the afternoon we ate corn *fufu* dipped in sauce. We ate separately as a family; you could take your dish and eat outside or inside, but often we ate inside to avoid the flies buzzing everywhere. It was especially hard to eat a sweet mango because the smell of mangos brought hordes of flies. We ate a lot of fruits, bananas, avocados, pineapple, and oranges. It was more common to eat fruit than meat. This is because we lived close to the tropical rainforest with banana trees and other kinds of fruit trees. The only time we ate meat was on special occasions like Christmas. But I was anemic, so I needed meat in my body.

My parents grew corn in a garden in the forest where people in the camp would farm. Our garden was not far away although it was a long walk when carrying a bag of corn over your head. When the corn was ripe, my mother and my sisters, Bebe and Niyo, would go out to pick the corn and return home carrying bags filled with stalks of fresh corn. First, they snapped the corn from the stalk and put them in sack bags, then after, we all sat down together in the yard to peel off the husks and lay the corn out in the sun to dry. I loved it when the corn was grilled.

The best part of the year was during the rainy season. The morning after a rain, everyone woke up early and went into the forest with glass containers to harvest the winged termites or *ishwa*. We  could only collect them during the insects' annual mating flight. At that time, we could catch them where they were flying low, some were on the ground. We would fill our bottles with *ishwa* and bring them back to the camp. There, we would strip off the wings and spread them out to dry. To prepare them, my mother would place them in a pan with a bit of salt and water and, stirring them constantly with a wooden spoon, cook them over a fire.

 They tasted delicious when fufu corn was dipped in them. I could never eat enough; I would keep going back in the kitchen for more. They re-placed the meat that we all longed for, but the winged termites are healthier than meat. They are rich in fat and protein. *Ishwa* were popular in the camp, particularly in shops where they were sold precooked.

I have nine sisters and brothers. I am the youngest boy and I have two younger sisters. Here is how I saw them when we were living in the camp.

I remember standing in the street, on a warm sunny day, and watching my two younger sisters playing hopscotch with two other children. The girl who threw a disk into a triangle and began jumping into space was born two years after me. Her name was Anika; she had short hair like most girls in the camp and wore a white dress. The one standing on the side waiting to see her sister mess up with her jumps was the youngest in the family. Her name was Ayana. Many families called their children by nicknames, and so Anika was called Hoza. The name was derived from the word *muhoza* which means a calm person. This name was perfect for her because she was a calm presence around the house. She was the oppo-site of me; I was clumsy and avoided other people. When we had visitors, I would run to hide in my playhouse to avoid them. Making eye contact with someone felt to me like they were shooting lasers at me through their eyes. While I struggled to deal with others, Hoza was completely different. She could stay on her feet, look people in the eye, and greet them without any fear. Even though Hoza was calm and brave most of the time, she still tended to cry a lot, crying over little things. Sometimes visitors assumed she was older than me. Perhaps because she seemed bigger and was almost the same height as me.

Hoza's younger sister Ayana was born a year after her; she was my youngest sibling. She had a sweet face, her eyes were lovely. Just looking at her brought me joy. She was also very kind. I can't remember a time she was angry or gave my mother a hard time. Unlike her older sister, she didn't receive a nickname. Although, I didn't think she needed one anyway because Ayana was already a beautiful name that described her well. Every time I said her name, it was like calling out the angels from heaven. As she grew, she was a little girl who loved to play with other children. She loved to laugh with the childlike wonder. She played with her sister Hoza, and they loved to walk around the neighborhood to find other children to play with. Hoza was always there for her. She was a shoulder for Ayana to lean on.

At an early age, it was clear to me that my relationship with Hoza and Ayana was stronger and more vital than all my siblings. This is mainly because I was accustomed to seeing them around the house playing with other children. I think they saw me as their big brother. When they were away in the neighborhood, I was the one who had to go find them when it was time to come home. One afternoon, I was at home playing in the mud like usual. I looked around the house and nobody was home. My consciousness had been situated in the mud; I had no idea I was alone. Suddenly my thoughts turned to my family's absence. It was too quiet, and I felt fear gushing out of my heart. I walked in the house and started yelling "Ma, Ma, Ma." A tear fell from my eyes as I called, "Fana, Fana, Ajani, where are you?" I walked back outside and searched around the neighborhood in hope of spotting somebody. I walked up the street as if I was searching for life. Then, on my right, I saw Hoza and Ayana playing hopscotch with other kids in front of their house. I called to them in a worried voice, "Go home, there is nobody at home right now." I felt like a big brother as I was urging them to return home, but I really just wanted their company. They were more willing to go to a stranger's house than me, I was wary of other people. Rugamba was perhaps the only person I was close to outside my family.

Our house only had two bedrooms for a big size house. Hoza, Anika, and I shared a room with our parents. My other sisters–Bebe, Niyo, Ajani, and Fana–shared a second bedroom. I was often at home alone while everyone else was wandering in the neighborhood. I felt frustrated, wondering where everyone was. Whenever I would ask my mother, "Where is Anika?" maybe it was loneliness speaking, but knowing where my siblings were made me feel better. I felt even better when everyone was at home.

There was often no real male figure around the house. My older brothers Desta and Ife, were rarely at home, just like my father. I didn't know much about them. To me, they were just older brothers in name but who were not intrinsically part of my life. I did want to know more about them; I thought they could somehow define my existence. However, I often felt fearful when I was with them. It was as if they were so detached and outside of my life that there was no way we were related. I felt more comfortable around my sisters. I loved listening to Bebe and Niyo talk. I would listen closely to their conversation. It brought me joy to be in the company of caring and loving sisters.

I remember watching the girl with a small and rounded head walking slowly and steadily towards my house while carrying a gallon of water over her head. She was my sister Ajani. She was born three years before I was born. She spent time with other girls who resembled her, standing in the street gossiping and giggling. She and I had a long history of being sick. She was also the only sibling who would get under my skin because she would make fun of me when I was clumsy and or acting weird. One day, I tripped and accidentally dropped my dinner on the floor while trying to talk to my mother. Ajani began to laugh at me with her annoying laugh. I was angry, so I threw a small rock at her, but she dodged it. I kicked the ground in frustration and walked away without picking up my dinner on the floor.

The teenage boy with a long neck and narrow shoulders, standing in the house and holding a notebook tightly to his chest, is Desta. He was born before Ajani. He is one of the six siblings who were born in Rwanda. Because he did not live with us but slept in his own house with his friends, I was too shy to talk to him. He would come to our house to eat and talk with our parents.

Desta cared about his education more than most; he learned to read and write, both some in French and a little bit in English. He had a small notebook with a brown cover which he carried with him every day. I didn't know what he was writing in the notebook, but I would watch him sitting alone in the house writing. It was like a diary. The notebook looked rather worn out, the cover falling apart, the pages loose, but Desta used tape and glue to mend the torn cover and pages. The notebook was almost always in his arms, but, every now and then, I would see it on the floor in the house, and I would pick it up and read through the pages. The writing was mostly in French which I could barely fathom; I struggled to read his handwriting because it was in cursive, and I was still learning cursive in school.

Desta loved to go to church; he was the first family member to choose to join the evangelical Pentecostal church. These believers did not drink alcohol and knew that they were the ones who had truly found God. Some members had begun to question the legitimacy of the Catholic Church and hoped to find salvation in the Pentecostal church. Desta was one of those who developed strong faith in Jesus after switching from Catholicism. He especially loved to sing in a choir with his friends. There were several Catholic churches in the camp but only one small building housed the Pentecostal church.

Desta was still young, about fourteen years old, when he left the Catholic church, but he had a sense of wisdom that distinguished him from most of his peers. When he was twelve, I used to hear Fana saying; "he is the same age as the twelve-year-old Jesus in Jerusalem." Even though every time he saw me while he was with his friends, he would immediately tell me to "leave and go home," I looked up to him as my big brother.

The girl with a calm look on her face, wearing a red shirt and rollers on her hair, and leaning down as she sweeps the yard with a straw broom is Fana. She is two years older than Desta. She was also well-read and educated like her younger brother. She was ahead in school and almost to secondary school. She was the one person to truly follow my father as a Catholic. She loved to attend the Catholic Church and she sang in a choir. I couldn't remember a time when she skipped going to church on a Sunday. The church was a big flat building with a roof and open on the sides so that you could see people sitting from outside. The priest was an old white man dressed in a white cassock. He could speak Kinyarwanda, which I found weird for a white person. I went to church almost every Sunday, and always on Christmas. Before the mass began, I would get to see kids moving through the aisles dancing; wearing the traditional African dancing garment, including *juju* dance anklets that jiggle as the dancer stomped. I tried-out to be one of the dancing kids with Rugamba, but we both failed to make the cut. I still recall the dance movement, the stomping particularly is still in my body. I would get to see my sister in a group of choirs standing in the front of the church wearing the traditional choir dress that was white and long like the clergy. They were singing the song "Gloria " in beautiful high, soprano voices that called for the angels from heaven. The church always decorated with flowers, candles, and the floor was covered with brown grass. Images celebrating Jesus's birth were hung on the wall. A large crucifix was displayed on the wall behind the altar. There were other images of Jesus and Mary carved in wood sculpture.

Fana had a gorgeous smile that showed her lovely cheeks. She also had big, healthy teeth. She loved to laugh a lot, but she was also prone to be easily irritated. I used to watch her and Ajani argue about house chores. I understood why she was often frustrated. They would argue about who was supposed to wash the dishes or clean the yard that was sometimes filled with mud and bricks from my playground. I could see distress on her face as she did her chores alone while her siblings were away in the neighborhood. Fana was a sister who cared about the family, she woke up every morning to sweep the yard. She also loved to knit; I would watch her every day sitting on a wooden chair at the front of the house knitting. She would make these beautiful lacey tablecloths with motifs. There were rectangular tablecloths and knitted with white and blue flowers.

Ife was a young man with a chin strap beard and a clean short haircut. He looked lean with denim black pants sagging down slightly from his waist. He was born a year after Fana, but, in those days, he was rarely seen. I used to think he was a mysterious brother. He was barely at home, too busy traveling and working outside of camp in the urban area of Ngara. I didn't even know that he was my brother until I saw him one day in our house. It was unusual to see him there. He had an impressive presence in our house because he was even bigger than my father. With his deep voice and charisma, he was respected by everyone in the family. He traveled all over

Tanzania, in cities like Dar es salaam. He was the only person in the family who could speak fluent Swahili. As he traveled, he grew to be an independent person. Sometimes he would bring things to us like food and money. He cared about me like a father, and every time he came home, he would notice me, and immediately give me something like a toy car or food. And yet, he never spoke to me. I used to hear that when he was a boy, he would build playhouses and create films for other children to watch, like a puppet show. He would take plastic containers and cut them into shapes of action figures. Then he would take a white trash bag and attach it to a small opening window to mask it as if it were a television. At night, he would turn on a light and take those action figures and perform with them on the "television screen." Viewers on the other side would see reflecting shadows of action figures fighting. As a boy, I started to follow in his footsteps, particularly by building small playhouses.

Niyo was a young woman when she was standing at the next-door house talking to her best friend Hawa. She was one of my oldest sisters. I could see her small eyes and chubby cheeks. I could also hear her familiar laughter; her laughter was grounded in the life of the camp, and it was filled with joy. Niyo was not only a people person, she was also an easy-going person who loved to talk about anything. She possessed a sense of wit, kindness, social presence, and laughter. Often, Hawa seemed to be a bad influence on Niyo; they loved to engage in all kinds of shenanigans, including secretly pouring a little spiciness in Hoza's breakfast drink and laughing about it. Teasing or pranking in the camp was sometimes harmful, but other times it was harmless, only for the sake of laughter.

Both Niyo and Hawa dropped out of school. Other young women married at a very young age and they never got the opportunity to further their education. But Niyo and Hawa just did not like school and rebelled against it. They had been brutally beaten by the teachers because they did not understand the lessons. But Niyo and Hawa would find joy in comedy. They would release their pain by transcending it in everyday laughter. For many young women in the camp, laughing was a form of coping mechanism in face of violence, hunger, and trauma. Niyo and other girls in the camp would travel a long distance into the forest to collect firewood. As they picked up or cut down what they needed in the nearby bushes, they would be wary of their surroundings. Any perceived movement from the forest bushes would cause panic; they feared being attacked or even killed. During the rainy season, they would trek through the mud and marshes carrying firewood over their heads. They would cross a river, with rising water levels from the rain. As they crossed the river, the water would often be shoulder deep. Most of them would be wearing flip-flops as they cautiously walked across the river, but not knowing what sharp rocks were hidden under the water.

Niyo loved helping around the house too. I would watch her washing clothes by hand in a basin filled with water and then scrub the clothes with soap. She would use fresh water to rinse the clothes and then hang the clothes on the clothesline to dry in the sun. I don't recall hearing her complaining about anything. While my other sisters, like Bebe and Fana, were constantly arguing and fighting over things, Niyo was the only one who remained quiet. She resembled her sister,

Hoza, with calmness and easy-going spirit. I aspired to be like her. For me, she was much easier to talk to than all my other siblings. But then, everyone loved to talk to her. The only times I felt excluded was when she was talking to friends and laughing about things I didn't understand.

The sister who was born after Niyo was Tina. She moved out and got married before turning 18 years old. I didn't know much about her because she was absent in my childhood, but Ajani used to go to her house to see her twin daughters.

Tina's older sister, Bebe, was tall. She was the oldest sibling and the first daughter my mother gave birth to. Bebe loved to dress in nice clothes every time she stepped outside in public. As a result, she could be high maintenance. I noticed this from how obsessed she was with her clothes and what people thought of her appearance. She wore tight jeans pants which, at this time, was rare for women in the camp. Nonetheless, Bebe was a very good person who loved to laugh and gossip like her sisters. When I saw her, she always had a smile on her face. She had a long face that resembled my mother and big shining teeth. She could speak a little bit of Swahili. When I was four years old and playing in the yard, sometimes she would call me, *Furaha*, which means happiness in Swahili. I was not sure why she was calling me that, but this was the way people would get nicknames by calling them a random name that is supposed to speak about their character or body image. I didn't know what *Furaha* meant since I didn't speak Swahili. The name stuck and became permanent. Furaha became the official name on my legal documents.

Bebe gave birth to a child named Liya while she was still

a teenager, living at home with us. As Liya grew, she seemed a bit confused about who her mother was–she would call her mother by her name, yet she called her grandma "mother". I watched her grow up as she learned to speak and become a child who loved to annoy me. She would destroy my play-houses and cry when I confronted her about it. But Liya was the best little niece I could've asked for. She loved to play with me by helping me build my playhouses.

The best family day was Christmas because we came to-gether on that day. There were no kids on the street playing; everyone was at home with their families. The entire neigh-borhood was feeling the mood of Christmas. Our living room was decorated with cut-out white paper flowers dangling on the ceiling like snowflakes. The three wooden chairs in the living room were covered with Fana's knitted chair covers. I felt joy seeing all my siblings–even Desta–at home. My Father, whom I rarely saw, was outside, comfortably sitting on a ladder-back chair next to the big tree; he was holding a radio in his hand, listening to a Christmas hymn, "Gloria in Excelsis Deo." The hymn was popular in the Catholic Church, and it was played in every home on Christmas.

Fana and Bebe were sing-ing along as they helped my mother prepare dinner. Ajani was sitting on a chair and facing the street while hand washing the dishes in the ba-sin. Niyo and Desta were sit-ting down on a blue and red

rug in front of the house, while holding a book together and singing a different hymn our mother loved.

Ai Mana y' ukuri,
komeza kunyobora,
Uranshishe mu nzira yo gukor' iby' ushaka
Mwami kubaho ntagufite
Binter' ubwoba n' amaganya
Ndetse byabasha kungeza no mu rupfu vuba
Ibyiza mbona n' ibi:
Kwizer' Umwami Yesu
No guhora ngendera mu nzira ye ntunganye
Nawe yemeye kujy' andinda,
Ndetse no ku nyobora neza
Ampesha no kwinjira vuba mu mahoro ye

O God of truth, continue to guide me,
You guide me in the way of doing what you want,
Lord, to live without fear and anxiety,
even if it could lead to death soon
The good things I see are these:
Believing in the Lord Jesus and always walking in his perfect way.
He has agreed to come to me, even to guide me well.
Help me to quickly enter into his peace.

Hoza and Ayana were not playing hopscotch; they were sitting in the house quietly waiting for dinner to be served. On special occasions like these, we had rice, cassava leaves sauteed in oil, and beef. I stopped playing in my playhouse and went to join them. I was feeling really excited, and I couldn't stop singing along to the song on radio "Gloria in Excelsis Deo," but in a rather mumbling manner because I couldn't understand the lyrics.

5

Boys in the Camp

I loved to play in the mud during the rainy season. The mud was soft, and I could feel it between my toes. I would spend hours building a small playhouse using bricks I found in the neighborhood. Or I would create my bricks by putting the mud into a mold over and over again. Then I would let the bricks dry in the sun. I would be so focused that I wouldn't hear my mother calling me to come in and eat. Sometimes I would build tiny houses, which allowed me to get more creative. I loved to recreate places I had been to like the hospital and store. I was able to rebuild the road that I walked on while going to the hospital. I built the hospital building with mud and the big chain-link face surrounding it by twisting small wires together.

I loved doing things alone. Sometimes other kids my age would join me. I felt angry inside when they insisted on playing with me because I would lose the joy of doing something by myself. But I didn't dare to ask them not to join. I had to pretend I enjoyed playing with them by holding back my feelings.

I remember when Rugamba, the one boy next door, asked if he could join me. "Can I play with you?" he said. I wanted to say no, but I saw the look on his face, he looked eager to play with me. I allowed him to help me make bricks, but slowly I was beginning to feel like I couldn't do things or express myself with another person. I started to feel his presence, his voice grew louder, his authority became excessive. I was no longer telling him what to do; he was telling me what to do. As we worked together drying more bricks, he kept talking more while I remained mute. When he started telling me how he would make the house, I knew my freedom was destroyed. "Stop adding more mud," he would say, when I knew more mud was needed. When we ran out of water for more brinks, he would tell me to take this rounded container and fill it with tap water or rainwater from the pit in the ground. I did everything he ordered me to do, but I didn't want to. I was afraid of talking back at him. I felt anxious around him, it was like my freedom was being threatened. I wanted to get rid of him, to tell him to leave me alone.

I thought he would stay away if I avoided him, so one day I locked myself inside the house all day. My mother was curious to know why I was sitting in the house. I was cooped up in the corner playing with one of my toy cars. She looked at me in bewilderment, "Why are you not outside?" she asked. I said nothing and kept slowly moving the toy car back and forth. She gave up on trying to understand me and went outside herself. A few minutes later, she returned to the house.

"Rugamba is outside waiting for you. He wants to play with you," she said to me. I was irritated, but I got up, walked outside, and saw him standing in the yard, waving his hand at me like he didn't know I was trying to avoid him. He loved to be around me, and I began to enjoy being with him. He grew on me.

One day Rugamba encouraged me to walk with him to an area in the camp I had never been to. Normally I would never even walk inches from home. We went to this place that was crowded with people, mostly adults. It was a busy place with people too absorbed in their normal activities. This was a market where people were selling and bartering goods. People selling clothes in small stores, others selling mangoes and bananas in baskets. Buyers, some walking, some on bicycles, were looking over the goods.. There were street kids called *mayibobo* in Kirundi, searching the ground for corn kernels and beans. They wore dirty, ripped clothes, and you can see hunger and desperation in their eyes. They had no place to go. We were glad we were not *mayibobo*.

There was a building with loud noise coming from inside. The noise was so loud, I could feel the ground shaking. People were standing around the door and waiting to enter. On the side of the building were movie posters. One of the posters had an image of a white man in a sleeveless denim shirt posing and holding two guns. When I came closer to the poster, I heard that his name was Chuck Norris.

White people were foreign human beings who lived different lives. There were many stories about them. It was said that their skin was softer than our skin. The white man in the poster didn't look anything like my father, but their beards were similar, so, I thought, that's why people called my father Chuck Norris. This experience with Rugamba made me realize how little I knew about the camp and what lay beyond.

When I was seven years old, I had been playing with Rugamba for a year. I was getting used to being in the company of another child. Although such a safe feeling would not last. One day, I was alone. I don't know where Rugamba was, maybe his mother needed him as she often did. It was midday and the sun was still in my face. I was sitting down pressing my feet in the mud when I felt two shadows moving towards me. I looked up and saw two boys. They lived in the neighborhood and they were much older than me. The tall boy on the left holding a wire toy car in his hand was John. He had cruel eyes and a sarcastic smile that intimidated me. The other boy's name was Aime, John's sidekick. John and Aime often made me do things for them as if I was theirs to command. I suppose I was a perfect target because I could not say no to anybody.

They would make me carry their clothes and wheel rims from bicycles which children in the camp played with by rolling it with a stick as they ran or jogged along. They also loved to expose their penises in front of me as a way to tease me and laugh at my discomfort.

On this day, as usual, they asked me to help them with something. They did not specify what they wanted me to do, but I was scared to refuse. We walked together to John's house, and as we arrived, a girl was waiting for them. John handed me his toy car. He held the girl's hand and then walked with her towards the small outdoor restroom composed of sticks and mud-built next to his house. He opened the restroom door and they went inside. A few minutes later, Aime followed inside with them, but before he entered, he told me to stand outside and guard the door. I was not sure what was going on inside the restroom. All I knew was that only one person was supposed to go into a restroom and not three. I sat down while leaning against the door. I could feel the restroom shaking. I was still sitting there and waiting for them to come out. I felt scared and foolish for sitting there with my heart racing, and trying to keep myself from crying.

Rugamba was a friend; John and Aime were not.

6

Illness and Diseases

Often when my feet started to feel itchy, I knew something was happening; it was the flea or *amavunja* as we would say. It was growing in one particular area under the skin of my foot and causing discomfort. The area was swelling with the egg growing inside the circle area. I couldn't put my weight on that spot when I was walking. My mother would take my foot and use a clean needle bought from a store to remove the egg inside of the area.

To protect ourselves from fleas, often we were encouraged to wash our feet and wear sandals. Not everyone could afford sandals, but some people refused to wear them because they thought they were created in Hell–a rumor that had spread throughout the camp. I was in bare feet most of the time when I was at home, but I had flip flop sandals. I wore them only to church and to shop with my mother.

Even though the United Nations provided food, we still

lived in hunger. There was also sickness in the camp. When I was about six- or seven-years old, I was infected with malaria. Common in tropical lands, malaria is caused a parasite that is spread by infected mosquitoes. The symptoms are fever, chills, vomiting, and pounding headaches. I can still recall the day I became ill.

It was afternoon, and I wanted to get out of the sun and sit in a shed beneath the big tree with long branches and a wide trunk that was growing next to our house. I had had a splitting headache all day which I thought was caused by the burning sunlight. After all, my mother was always encouraging me to not stay in the sun for too long. As I sat leaning against the tree, I felt shooting pain in my muscles. The headache continued to get worse like a tight band around my head. I started to feel fatigued, my arms and body felt heavy. I was feeling chill. I knew I was getting sick, and I thought I needed my mother. I wanted to cry because the pain was unbearable. My mother was nowhere in sight. "Ma, Ma," I cried in a harsh and painful manner. I went into the house looking for my mother. Fana was sitting there, knitting. "Where is Ma?" I asked her. She looked at me with concern, "She is at the store. Are you okay? You look sick." "I am not feeling well," I answered while walking back outside, feeling dizzy.

I sat down resting against the front of the house, shivering and shaking. I felt like throwing up, feeling something tightly down in my throat and belly, and asking to be released from my body. I waited to let go like I was about to sneeze and suddenly I began to vomit and vomit and vomit. I couldn't stop. My mother arrived home and ran to me. She touched my forehead. "You are burning," she said. She took me inside and lay me down on the bed. Later, she helped me to drink some soup.

The next day when I was no better, my mother took me to the hospital. I remember that it was a bright, sunny morning, but as we were walking and I was holding onto my mother's hand, I was shivering and my head felt like it would break into pieces. We were walking slowly on the sidewalk of the dusty road when a car drove by causing a dust wind. The hospital was located outside the camp; it smelled like the sickness that was upon me. The doctor told my mother that I was suffering from malaria. I was relieved because at least I had the chance to recover. I was given medication to fight the parasite, but I was unlucky to have long-term malaria that caused me to be anemic and have headaches long after I had recovered from the worst symptoms.

7

Nelson Mandela School

I never really liked school. I just wanted to stay at home and build my playhouses. The six-hour school day felt so long; I was exhausted. No time brought me more joy than the last minute of a school day; to hear the whistle that freed me and allowed me to go home.

We were provided with schools for all ages in the camp. There was a pre-school for four- and five-year old kids, but serious school started in primary school from first grade to fifth grade. The school was called "Nelson Mandela School" to honor the South African social crusader. The school consisted of multiple buildings that looked like a long rectangular shape that stretched out in a square like the structure of the prison on Robben Island where Nelson Mendela was held for 27 years as he fought for his freedom.

Built of bricks and sand from the ground up, the buildings had small, squared windows and metal roofs.

To pass to the next grade, each student had to earn a particular score on a test. On the last day of the year, parents were required to come to class with their children and hear the teacher call the names of students who passed or failed. The score started from first to twenty. A student whose name was called first was the best student. The last to be called was considered to be the worst student in the class. I never failed a class; I would always finish between six or seven, which was good enough.

Some students would fail to pass a class and be held back in the same grade for another year. It was possible to be in the class with someone five years older than you. I thought this is why so many students were dropping out of school; they did not want to keep repeating the same lessons year after year. The older students who stayed in school loved to sit at the back of the class. Because they were older and bigger than the rest of the class, they would bully the younger ones. They enjoyed throwing things at the quiet kids like me, knocking on the back of a kid's head like the teachers loved to do, or slap a kid hard on the back shoulder. It was torture to be in class. You would sit in class, wary of people sitting behind you, and hoping that nobody would touch you that day.

When I was in third grade, we were taught French, Math, and Kirundi. Math was essential, and some students struggled with it. We learned Kirundi because many of us only spoke a mixed dialect language using Kirundi and Kinyarwanda. The difference between the two languages was mostly wording and pronunciation. It was spoken by kids who had parents who had lived in Rwanda for a long time. But the truth was that the school was organized by the Burundian government as an effort to provide education to dislocated Burundians in the camp.

When the bell rang, students would quickly line up two-by-two at the door. One of my biggest fears had been being with other kids. They made me feel nervous and shy. I also rarely made eye contact with people. I remember being in a classroom with kids jumping and screaming as the teacher tried to keep them under control. I was one of the kids who sat quietly in the corner and kept looking at the ground with shyness and fear painted on my face. I had not moved my lips for the entire school day. I was terrified.

The teachers were very strict. They did not care how old a student was. They would yell at you if you made a mistake and hit you on the back of your legs with a stick. I had a lot of whip marks on my legs. This approach of teaching was effective because many of us worked hard to learn and to avoid mistakes and getting hit. But sometimes each of us had to take the hit. My third-grade teacher was a woman in her mid-30s; she was slim and tall with a long nose and large upper teeth that showed as she spoke. If she asked a question such as, "What is 5+7?" and nobody responded, she would look around to pick someone to answer the question. I was always scared that she would call on me. Her eyes would glance quickly around the room, like a gun pointing at us. We had to look her in the eyes because if you looked away, you were likely to get picked for being distracted. I was scared to blink my eyes as I stared at her. If she picked this random boy, he would be sweating with fear. If his answer was wrong, she would ask him to come forward and tell him to face away. Then she would grab a branch stick and begin hitting it on his legs or back. You would see tears in the boy's eyes as he dealt with the pain. We all sat and watched. It was a normal thing that happened to each of us when we were unlucky.

Sometimes kids would tease me and push me around. Some of the boys even thought I was a girl because of how shy I seemed. Most of the boys were very energetic; I was more thoughtful. I would avoid other boys by sitting in a corner alone. I felt there was something wrong with me, but I didn't know what it was.. Often when I was alone at home, I would contemplate the problem of my difference. Do the other boys act differently when I am not around? Is there something about being a boy that I don't know? Is it something they are not telling me? Why do I feel so different? Why am I so alone? The other boys played complicated games with rules I couldn't grasp. The others were beings whose existence, I felt, I didn't deserve to share.

One day during recess all the kids were outside playing. The playground had a long trench to catch rainwater, but it was often dry. It was neither too wide nor too not deep, so kids could easily jump in and climb out of it. The kids would run around in it, and I sometimes joined, but it was mostly boys there, filled with lots of energy. One time in the pit, I was caught by three boys who approached me thinking I was a girl. They seemed surprised to find a girl in the pit. "Furaha, Furaha," one of the boys called. They shoved me against the side of the pit and began laughing. One of the boys pulled my shorts down to see how I looked between my legs. They were disappointed to find out I shared the same gender. I had a penis. The disappointment on their faces terrified me; disappointed, they looked at me and slapped me in the face. They begin to touch my penis by squeezing it hard. "Is God watching? A boy is being assaulted," I wondered as they turned and ran away. I cried to myself as I walked away deeply upset by what just happened.

Moments like this brought fear into my heart, and school represented long stretches of anxious hours. I hated school so much that I began to skip school. I would spend most of the days in my playhouse and grinding my teeth in sadness. Finally, my older brother Ife forced me to go to school, dragging by pulling my shirt. "You need to go to school," he said. I resisted the force by dragging my feet. So he dragged me like a heavy chair. I understood why Ife wanted me to go to school—he himself had dropped out of school at a young age to earn money, but he had come to regret that decision. I think he didn't want to see me going on the same path, but all I wanted to do was to stay at home and build my playhouses.

Even though I resisted, attending school was very important for my development. I needed to be around other kids to grow and learn. All the other kids were going to school. When I was still in 3rd grade, my friend Rugamba was in 4th grade, and he could speak a little French. I was doing well myself, and Rugamba and I would study French together after school. One time we were sitting together outside my house. Rugamba was just returning from school; he had his French book with him. He took it out of his arm, sat down next to me, and opened the book.

"J'ai mal à la têteto," he read from his book.

"What does that mean?" I asked?

"It means 'I have a headache'," he said.

Rugamba was a smart boy, but I didn't see him as much

at school. I wanted to tell him about what happened to me at school but decided to remain quiet.

I asked my mother about how I could deal with bullies at school. I thought that my mother had all the answers. I loved asking her all kinds of questions, including why my father was barely ever at home. But even though I asked, she rarely answered my questions, unless it was something regarding my relationships with other children. She taught me this: If I could carry on with my own life, I could be free from hours of bitterness and fear. I took this advice seriously, and every day I was in school, I kept these thoughts in mind.

"Walk with courage, and let your heart be controlled by you but not someone else. Pray to God and be good," my mother would counsel me. Every word she uttered seemed to shape my life. "I am my own joy," I thought. "I can smile alone without being affected by other voices that attempt to make me change my personality and character. I would rather live in the mind of God."

And so I chose to go to school to find joy in knowledge —not to waste my time worrying about what other people think. Unfortunately, before I could start living the words, the schools in the camp were beginning to shut down as people began leaving to find new lives in different countries.

8

My Beautiful Angel

We were still living in the isolated camp in Tanzania when the discord and strain among the residents exploded into violence. People began poisoning one another over deep-seated anger. Poison could be in the food your neighbor gave you when you were hungry. If you ate too much of the food, the poison stayed in your body to suffocate you.

My sister Ayana didn't know better; she was just hungry like most of us. After she ate the toxic food, her sickness caused her to throw up black vomit which was bloodied from the poison. But she could not clear out enough from her stomach to save her.

She and Hoza were out in the neighborhood as usual, but this time they were sitting at the next-door neighbor's yard. Rugamba, who lived there, was not home. Despite being my childhood friend, I had never eaten food at his house or talked to his mother. This is why I was shocked to see Hoza and

Ayana in the morning drinking igikoma at his house, with his mother standing beside them. My mother didn't want us to trust everyone in the neighborhood, but I was the only one who listened to her.

Later, we could never prove that Rugamba's mother did anything to harm my sisters, but it seemed so to me.

I didn't think there was anything wrong, but I was not comfortable seeing them drinking something that was not provided by our mother. Hoza didn't like the taste, so she put the mug on the ground and told Ayana to stop drinking. She thought something was wrong. But Ayana kept drinking.

The next day, I saw that both were sick. Ayana was coughing a lot, and Hoza looked tired and unwell. They were vomiting every minute like they were releasing something inside that was tightly holding on to them. I couldn't bear to look at the pain they were in. I had never seen them like that. The two girls who normally ran around, jumping and laughing, had become ghosts in my sight. It was haunting and too quiet all day at home. Each day they would get worse, and they were asleep all day. Ayana couldn't even walk. When neighbors came to help take Ayana and Hoza to the hospital on the bicycle, I knew something was seriously wrong. Even I felt weak and lifeless. I could smell fear everywhere around the house. I saw fear in the eyes of all my sisters and brothers. My mother went to the hospital with them and stayed beside them. I learned that Hoza recovered because she had vomited up the poison, and she returned home looking healthy. Unfortunately, Ayana was still at the hospital. My mother was sitting on her bed, praying for her recovery, but her pain was not abated. She was not coming home soon.

I don't know why they took her away. She was so young and innocent. She had kind eyes that gazed into my soul. My memory of her still haunts me.

The last time I saw Ayana alive and healthy, she was with Hoza playing in the neighbor's backyard, laughing with joy and running away from bees with other children. Ayana came home complaining to our mother that she had been stung by a bee.

My last memory of my little sister was lovely. It was raining hard outside. Ayana with her eyes of innocence had run outside in the rain. I recall calling her to come back inside, but she seemed to be enjoying herself. She was laughing and dancing while spreading her arms up. She tilted her head up to the sky to catch the falling rain. She laughed again, drinking drops of rain. I remember her laughter like yesterday. It was as sweet and lovely as listening to an angel. It was not mere laughter, it was the laughter of a child who has been touched by love from heaven.

I was sitting down in the front of the house with all my sisters and brothers as we waited to hear the news. Fana was looking down with her hands clasped tightly together. When the news of Ayana's death arrived, it filled up the space where we all had been anticipating. My mother arrived at home alone, with her hands on her chest and trying to hold back tears. "She is gone," my mother said in a harsh and weakened voice. Everything stopped. Fana was the first to hit the ground on her knees in agony. I couldn't believe what I was hearing, so I rubbed my eyes to see if I was dreaming. I walked inside of the house feeling confused. I looked back outside and saw Ajani crying heavily. I sat on the chair in the living room with my arms folded to my chest, I doubted her death, but my mother had her hands pressed on her face in pain. Bebe was crying too. Niyo, who was always happy, was sobbing loudly. Hoza ran inside crying and almost bumped into me. I returned outside, leaned against the wall on the front of the house, and put my hands over my head. My body felt weak down to my knees. I whimpered and instantly tears began rushing down my cheeks, and I dropped down on the ground crying. I felt I will never stop crying until she comes back to life. Our house was the sound of weeping.

She was away for good.

I saw her body; it was covered in a blanket with green and yellow stripes. She was borne on the shoulders of neighborhood men to the cemetery. I heard the people singing a hymn that is still today in my mind—I think my mother used to sing it, "Imana Yagiziki ngwino Kibondo Caje," "God Did This, Come to Me, My Child." I hoped that she had traveled to heaven as I had been taught by my parents. Her absence brought many questions that echoed back without answers–a sound of nothing. Now her life existed only in my mind and her mode of being was nonexistent. The fact that I would never hear her laugh again caused me to cry with horror; the horror was the reality of death. The idea of not seeing her again was torture. Even today, she never ceases to be far from me–she is always in my mind. . . .

My beautiful little sister was a bright angel. When I cried, every teardrop was a reminder that she was in my heart.

9

Starting Over

In the next few days of grief, we were all sad. My father who was normally working was unusually at home in the morning. He didn't look like himself; he did not only have a grieving face, he looked fatigued and unwell as well. I had never seen my father looking that way. Even though he was a large, robust man, he was always doing something. But now, I would see him coughing in the morning and sleeping in all day. It was nice to see him in the house more, but not this way. Suddenly my mother began to cough. I thought she had been infected by my father. But everyone at home was sick except Ife who was still traveling. I couldn't eat anything without throwing up. "Something weird is happening, we are all getting sick," said Fana. It felt like the pain of Ayana's death was coming to haunt us. Looking around the house with a headache and a shivering body, I couldn't believe what was happening. Was Ayana calling us to follow her from heaven, I wondered. My mother who was normally busy taking care of us looked too sick to help me. Ajani was vomiting with tears running down her face. Hoza, who had just recovered, was sick again. It took about two weeks for everyone to recover.

I saw my step-brother Wira, a tall, slim middle-aged man, standing outside of the house and talking to my father. Wira was telling my father that he had recently found a house nearby where his family and including his mother lived. The next thing I remember is that my parents were urging us to pack our things and get ready to move. Our new house was better than our previous one. It looked strong and well built with bricks. All the reasons for moving were unclear; the house was bigger and more solid than ours but my parents kept the move a secret and didn't want to make it obvious to the neighbors. But most of us knew we were moving because we wanted to get away from something, and the something was not doing us any favor. I never learned what the secret was.

Moving into a new house meant moving into another neighborhood. Our new house was built below a big steep hill that everyone had to walk up through to get to the store or to get food or aid. It was exhausting to walk up the hill, but it was fun to see kids using wooden sleds to slide down the hill. I missed Rugamba a lot. I was returning to my normal activity which was building a playhouse. But my new playground was smaller; I had limited space to play because the yard on the side of the house was occupied with trees and tall grass. There was something different about me. I was deeply lost in sadness, not talking to my siblings, and not immersed in my usual activities, but simply longing to be alone.

Travis was a crazy looking kid with a mischievous character who lived next door behind my house. He was tall for his age and had a dark skin tone. He wanted to be my friend which I thought was bizarre because we had different personalities. He came to talk to me one time while I was playing in my playhouse. I learned from my family that Travis was raised without a father, but had a kind older sister who unfortunately had HIV. As I looked into his eyes, I could smell bad news. He started telling me about a girl across the street with whom he had sex in the restroom. I was horrified, not for having sex with this girl, but for telling me. I was only eight years old and anything involving sex made me uncomfortable.

At that time, I had no idea how sex worked, but they were several incidents in my life that suggested that it was a bad thing. My siblings had told me that there was a creepy old man in the neighborhood who walked around pretending to play with children and lifting them up, but then pulling his penis out while holding them close to his groin area. Another incident was when I started to feel ashamed for allowing girls to play with me in my playhouse. There was a rumor going around in the neighborhood about a girl who was caught engaging in sexual activities with another boy. After hearing about it, I remember feeling like the boy could have been me. I had no problem playing with girls until that moment. I was ashamed of being a boy despite not knowing how sex worked. I thought sex was a penis pushed into a girl's belly. Older boys would use cut-out figures from plastic containers for sexual means. One of these figures was a boy with a cut-out penis and another was a girl with what seemed to be a cut-out shape of a triangle cut inside her groin. The penis would push inside the triangle. I couldn't fathom why such activity was so appealing or consequential. In my mind, sex was becoming something vulgar and shameful.

Travis was older and bigger than I was. He would encourage me to go to all kinds of places in the camp. We would walk around the school campus, sitting in an empty classroom and writing insulting things on the board.

One evening, I could see the sunset from a distance. I was going to the hospital with Travis and his other friends. I thought we were just hanging around. Travis told me that they wanted to break into the hospital by going under the tall chain-link fence with its barbed wire. I told Travis that I didn't want to go, but he kept insisting that I join them. I remember running back home with my heart beating fast as the sunset kissed my timid face. I knew Travis was a bad influence on me. It became more evident when my mother told me that he had stolen new soap bars from my house. I was confused about how Travis got into my house.

I was doing everything I could to avoid Travis. He tried to talk to me multiple times while building my playhouse. He would stand in front of me and as he spoke to me, I could tell he wanted to be on my good side so we could hang out again. "I am sorry about the soap, we should go to the store," he said, smirking. Just listening to him made me miss Rugamba even more. I would sometimes go back to my old neighborhood to see Rugamba. I experienced a sense of nostalgia as I stared at my old house and where I used to build my playhouse. I almost shed a tear when I looked at the big tree that I used to lean on. I felt warm tears in my eyes caused by melancholy remembrance.

10

"I want to go"

It was evening, and we were eating dinner outside as a family. Sitting separately in front of the house with our plates balanced in our laps, we were talking quietly with one another. I was enjoying the strong smell of the rich and nourishing white cooked rice. I was sitting with my shoulder leaning against the front of the house as I ate my rice and beans. Suddenly, something happened at the moment, but I don't recall what caused it to happen. Something snapped inside my mind and I felt an overwhelming fear. I remember screaming and crying. My mother and Fana were holding me, trying to keep me from slipping out of their arms. I was angry, I was fearful.

"Leave me alone! I want to go," I cried. I was screaming at the top of my lungs. Neighbors rushed outside to witness the scene. I was surrounded by people holding my hands and trying to keep me calm. I kept screaming, "I want to go! I want to go! I want to go!" Soon the entire neighborhood was outside, watching my insanity.

I was later taken to hospital. My mother was still holding my right hand and three men were tightly holding me close as we walked. I slept on the hospital bed that night and woke up the next morning, feeling calm again. I have little recollection of the evening, but I still keep wondering why I was screaming, "I want to go!" Why did I want to go? Where did I want to go?

11

The Lure of the United States

By 2006, the quality of life in the refugee camp was deteriorating. For decades, Tanzania had a policy of open asylum for refugees from neighboring lands, primarily Burundi. In the early days, Tanzania offered land to refugees, encouraging the development of sparsely populated areas and increased international aid to the region. Overall, 162,000 Burundians became naturalized citizens of Tanzania. However, as the flow of refugees increased, international aid decreased, and security problems escalated, other "durable solutions" to the refugee issue were being explored. The Tanzania government began to pressure refugees to leave by closing down support, such as the schools and markets, within the camps. By 2006, our camp Ngara had no schools and no police protection. Children were left adrift and crime, particularly theft, was increasing. It was time to leave.

For Tanzania, the preferred solution, of course, was re-patriation of refugees, and many did return to Burundi. As long as the refugees had family ties, land or some kind of wealth there, and were not perceived as a threat to the ruling party, repatriation was possible. Those Burundians who had fled the country during the ethnic violence that broke out in 1993 typically faced fewer problems in reclaiming their land. Despite the unstable political situation within Burundi, more than 50,000 Burundian refugees returned home in 2005. On the other hand, if the refugees had fled from Burundi during the "Great Calamity" of 1972, as my family had done, their ties to the homeland had faded so that returning to Burundi thirty years later was not a real possibility. We would not have survived there.

Another division among the refugees lay in the age differ-ences. The older generations, parents and grandparents, were longing to return home. But the young Burudians who had been born in Tanzania had no memories of Burundi, so most of them had no desire to return to a country they never even thought about. These young people perceived themselves as Tanzanian; they had been raised in Tanzanian culture, their friends were Tanzanians, and their lives resided in Tanzania. Also, given the deeply rooted patriarchal society in Burundi, it was difficult for young women to have access to education there. As a result, many young Burundian refugees preferred to stay in Tanzania.

The only other solution for my family was emigration.

I recall Desta and Fana talking about the possibility of

going to France; this prospect excited Desta who loved everything about France, including the French national soccer team which had just been defeated by Italy in the FIFA World Cup final. Most soccer fans in the camp supported the French national team because of our connection to the language. Desta didn't just love soccer, he also loved the culture in France.

Some of our neighbors were returning to Burundi, and their houses looked deserted. Others managed to obtain visas to enter Australia and the United States, but we knew that these neighbors had lied to the immigration officials about facing death threats or other dangers, and my parents would not lie.

In October 2006, we heard the best news of our lives. The United States had agreed to resettle 13,000 refugees living in camps under a UNHCR resettlement program. The offer was guaranteed to Burundian refugees who had fled in 1972 and settled in Tanzania camps. Happily, my family met those requirements.

The processing of refugees was getting underway during the month of October. Interviews were held in the camps of Kasulu, Kisulu, Kibondo, and Ngara. We didn't know when we were expected to fly to the United States, but it was estimated that the process would take at least two years because there was a large group of people involved.

Not long after my outburst, I was standing outside in front of my house, gazing down on the street. I had been feeling ashamed for the last few days; I couldn't go outside because I didn't want neighbors who witnessed my outburst to see me. I thought they might think that I was "the crazy boy who was screaming". Yet, on this day, I was not ashamed to be stared at by the neighbors. I thought maybe my emotional break-down was forgotten, and I was feeling great. I saw my mother walking down the hill, and I felt relieved to see her. It was another sunny afternoon, but there was a changed attitude in the camp, an uneasiness shared by everyone.

There was a middle-aged woman next door who used to greet my mother; every day, she would say, "*Mwaramutse mama Bebe*"-- "Good afternoon, Mama Bebe." On this day, though, the woman was sitting on a wooden stool washing clothes with her eyes lost in her chores, and she didn't look up to greet my mother. There was gloominess on her face as she focused on washing the clothes in the basin.

The streets were filled with children running around; I saw a group of girls playing hand-clapping games and boys running after each other like they had nothing better to do. I could feel a sense of boredom in my heart as I stared at the kids. I felt that, just like those boys in the street, I had no structure in my life because we were no longer attending school. Even though I had so much time to build my play-house, I would feel something sharp in my heart, scratching me when I didn't have anything else to do. I picked up a small skin care bottle lying on the ground; I assumed it belonged to my sisters. I looked at it and saw an image of a woman with long straight hair and light skin complexion. I was puzzled because I couldn't distinguish if she was black, arabic, or white. I had so many questions racing in my mind, they were hurting me.

My mother looked tired as she arrived at home. "Mom,

where are you coming from?" I asked as I followed her into the house.

"I am returning from an immigration interview." My mother was a hard-working person. She did everything for the family. While my father was busy with his job, my mother played the role of head of household; she was responsible for knowing and keeping information about our immigration status.

For the past few months, the country that caused the most tension and envy among people in the camp was the United States. Who would be chosen to emigrate? Almost everyone in the camp who applied as part of the 1972 refugees group was in the process of interviewing. For many people in the camp who had no way of returning to Burundi, the United States was their last resort. The biggest concern among those being interviewed was who could tell the simple truth about the 1972 flight from Burundi or the Rwanda genocide that occurred later without elaborating? Who could speak about their family situation without becoming too emotional and losing control. It was dangerous to start to rant, tell too many details, and reveal deep-seated anger. It was dangerous to declare political positions. Every person's goal in their immigration interview was to simply tell about fleeing the genocide and nothing else. Keep the story simple; don't tell too much.

When decisions were made about who was chosen, we would find out by reading white paper lists that were posted on the sides of buildings in the busy market area and on tree trunks. People would gather around to read the list of people who qualified to go to the United States. I used to see people walking away from the crowd in a mournful manner, looking as if they had just witnessed some kind of horror. Others would jump in the air and yell, "Thank you, God! We are going to the United States!" Parents would run home in a hurry to tell their kids the good news. I remember clearly that day when my mother told me that we had qualified.

12

The New Camp

In the Ngara refugee camp, it was rare to see a car in the neighborhood. Whenever there was a car on the street, kids would chase after it, screaming in excitement. The older kids would jump onto the back of a moving car for a ride. I remember that the cars were white, and at night I was fascinated with the rear red flashing lights. These cars belonged to UNICEF; they came to the camp a few times in the year to collect documents like birth certificate records from the refugees chosen to go to the United States.

For those who looked forward to riding in a motor vehicle, the chance soon came. Family groups were being taken by bus to a new camp in Tanzania to prepare to emigrate to the United States. We were among those who rode in the crowded bus to settle in this new camp. Not all members of my family made the trip. My parents, Hoza, Fana, Ajani, Ife, and Desta were all on the bus with me. Niyo, who was over the age 18, became independent because of the immigration rule, so she had already arrived in the camp ahead of us. Bebe was also independent and still raising Liya alone; eventually, they emigrated to Canada.

On the bus, my parents were sitting together. It was scary to be in a moving object; I was sitting next to Hoza and holding tightly onto my seat with fear we might fall. We were not provided any food, but my mother had packed roasted corn in a bag for us to eat. Some people were becoming sick with the motion of the bus. It was a long drive to the new camp. I tried not to look down because every time I did, I threw up. It was safe to look out of the window. We were moving past mountains and shelters, but as we continued moving, I felt the ghost of Ayana running after the bus, crying in despair.

 As we stepped off the bus, anticipating a brief new life there before flying to the United States, we stood on the ledge staring down at the camp. It was located in the middle of a forest in terraced rows beneath a hill, but it was more settled and developed than the Ngara refugee camp. There were terraced houses built with orange and red bricks and metal roofs. Each house had a door and a wooden framed window facing the front. There was a restroom built next to each house. For the first time, my family was living in a house that they had not built with their own hands

I was growing skinnier. I was not sure why, but I didn't have an appetite at first. I thought that perhaps I was missing Rugamba. There was a small round mirror on the floor in the living room. I picked it up and began using it to study my face. As I looked closely into my reflection, I hated my facial appearance–particularly my cheeks, they were too chubby. But I loved the fact I was skinny because I thought I looked taller as I looked at my shoulders and my flat chest. I was sadder and lonelier than usual. My lips were drier and, often I did not talk to anyone all day long. I would weep for no reason while sitting in the yard looking up at the clouds, gentle and melancholy tears.

I could still build a playhouse. Finding children to play with was hard. I had not seen Rugamba since the tragedy. I was now far away from him in a new camp. There was no school, so most kids were bored living at home and waiting for their family to be called on to fly to the United States.

In the neighborhood, there was a boy who shared my last name, Nsengiyumva. In the camp, Burundian people were called by their last names which were either Rwand-Rundi (Rwandan or Burundian). All the names had meaning, many of them are faith-based such as Sabimbona (*I ask God who sees me*) or Nizigiyimana (*I hope in God*). My last name is Nsengiyumva, meaning *Praying while I Listen*.

I saw the boy walking near my house with his little brother. His family lived two houses from my house. They were close to our family because we had known them in our previous camp. He wore black pants that were wide on the bottom. I couldn't forget the way he walked–his swinging arms would casually match with his stepping legs. We would spend time together with other kids in the neighborhood, walking in the forest or swimming in the swamp. I was only eight years old, the youngest in this group. Some of the kids would laugh at the size of my penis as we stripped off our clothes to jump into the dirty, swampy water. I was still very shy, so these taunts hurt me. I felt worthless next to these older and bigger kids. They gave me a nickname to avoid having two people with the same name. They started calling me "Songyeye, "Songyeye, "Songyeye," a kind of sing-songy, silly name. When I heard it, I felt like being shot in the chest. I thought the name was hurtful, but I was too afraid to say anything back. Eventually, I decided that maybe I deserved it since I was not as good-looking and likable as the other boy named Nsengiyumva.

I was no longer sleeping in the same room with my parents, I slept alone in the living room while my sisters slept together in a separate room. Desta and Ife were still living separately with their friends. I was scared of the dark. I would keep the small string lights that required batteries on all night. I kept my eyes open looking at the door in case somebody might break in. Sometimes it was better to turn the lights off to avoid sleeping with eyes open.

I was also scared of animals, particularly cats. They terrified me with their big rounded eyes, which I thought stared deep into my soul. I also hated the fluffy hair and the whisker hair around their nose. Most animals were not treated like pets in the camp although some people loved cats and were able to keep them as pets. However, most animals, especially dogs, were not friendly pets. Most dogs in the camp were not trained as pets, they were either trained to hunt or they ran wild. Whenever people encountered an unleashed dog, they would run for safety. The dogs were aggressive–they would run wildly after you barking and howling. And they would bite people. One day I saw kids in the neighborhood, standing in front of an empty house and beating a dog to death. Nobody protested or asked them to stop; it was the normal thing people do.

One day, Hoza told me, "There is a cat in the house." A small white cat was hiding in there, and I was scared to go inside. Finally, Ajani and I tried to get rid of it because we both hated cats. Ajani thought cats were gross. She walked into the house slowly, but the cat was in our parent's bedroom and hiding under the bed. I was right behind her, feeling scared. Ajani tapped on the bed hard, and suddenly the cat rushed out quickly and ran outside. I was relieved at first, but then we found that there was cat poop on the floor under the bed. Ajani didn't want to pick it up. She came back outside and told me to grab the white shirt hanging on the clothesline. I knew it was a shirt Fana used to wear for school, but she was traveling in Kigoma. I took the shirt from the clothesline, but as I handed it to Ajani, I was not sure why she needed it. Fana returned home a few days later. The first words I heard from her were, "Who put poop on my shirt?" I looked at her furious face while holding back my laughter. Despite the funny side of it, I knew it was the wrong thing for Ajani to use Fana's shirt to pick up the cat poop.

There was an Anglican church in the new camp. A group of refugees who wanted to continue their religion had built the church. It was a small building located on the edge of the camp where people had also built a small market. The products in the market were similar to those in our previous camp–mangoes, bananas, clothes spread out on the tables. One day, when I was with my mother, she bought me a green, striped, button-down shirt and denim pants. I wore the shirt the next morning when we were preparing to go to church. Hoza was wearing her light green dress. I was still yet to button a shirt. Fana asked Hoza and me to sit on the chair in front of the house for a photo. Fana joined us and sat next to Hoza while knitting her tablecloth. "Get ready," said Yvonne, holding a Polaroid digital camera. Yvonne didn't want to join us, but she was happier to take the photo. Sitting next to Hoza made me feel like we were twins because she looked like she was the same age as me. After posing for the photo, we walked together to the Anglican church. As we walked, my mother was beside me with Hoza and Ajani. Niyo, who looked like she was gaining weight, was right behind us. Fana stayed home knitting. There was no Catholic Church in this camp which was unfortunate for Fana, so she spent a lot of time doing chores.

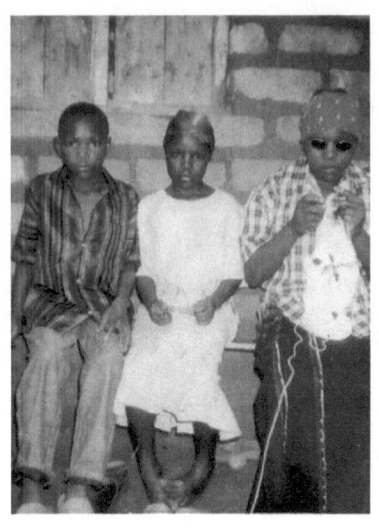

We were beginning to go to church more. My mother would encourage me and Hoza to attend church every Sunday. The church was small with only about twenty people in it. The Anglican church was kind of similar to the Protestant Church in that we sang the same songs and there was communion rather than eucharist. A Tanzanian priest would often come for special events like baptisms. The pastor who preached every Sunday was a man from the camp who always wore a black clergy shirt. As we worshiped, we sang songs that were joyful and incredibly touching. Ajani, Hoza, and I were in the choir with other children. We had choir rehearsal every Saturday. Since we didn't have school, being part of a choir provided me with something to do other than constantly building a playhouse. Singing was not something I felt comfortable doing, so I sang softly with shyness. But as I continued to sing with the choir, I gradually started to raise my voice. It was a relief because I couldn't even hear my voice. Other kids who were mostly girls, had a higher singing tone. I felt like I didn't feel like I needed to raise my voice to be heard.

After months attending church, the day finally came: my siblings and I, as well as other children were baptized by the Tanzanian priest. All the kids in the choir walked steadily to the front of the church. The priest was wearing a white robe and blue scarf called a stole. The pastor was standing next to the priest holding an open bible. When it was my turn, I

stepped in the front and stood at the altar with my hands clasped in front. I was shaking as the priest placed his cold, wet finger on my forehand and recited something I don't recall. I was baptized. I saw my mom smiling.

13

The Dread of Night

During our two years in this new camp, we had no formal education. To prepare to become Americans, we were told to support the principles and ideals of the Constitution of the United States, and we were asked to take an oath of allegiance to the United States. We were told to be good citizens and follow the laws. I remember we were told to not engage in political organization against the United States or any communist organization.

Overall, there was a sense of jubilation in the house. It was evening, and I could see the sunset. We were all sitting outside of the house eating dinner. I was holding a bowl of rice and eating it with my clean hand. Hoza, Fana, Ajani, and Desta were also there eating. Desta was talking about this person who was running for president in the United States and how he was about to be the first black president of the United States. His name was Barack Obama. Desta was so desperate to fly to the United States, he couldn't stop talking about it.

I didn't know anything about the United States, I barely knew a word of English. People used to say that in some parts of the country, there are white stuff that would fall from the sky. We were familiar with American movies such as *Rambo* and *Spiderman*. It was soon to be our new country. Everyone was excited about the possibility of leaving this hardship of life in refugee camps behind. My sisters were beginning to grow their hair, imitating the more open culture by wearing pants and learning a little English. Desta, who was well-read, was already an expert about the country, so he would share with us a little of his knowledge. "There are tall buildings with five or six floors," he told us, describing a place called New York and its skyscrapers. There was something alien about what he was saying, but I couldn't wait to put my foot on this shining land. We had a few days left before flying to the United States. We were all excited to see this day, but that didn't stop us from enjoying the new things that were being presented to us.

In the camp, we were provided with an outdoor movie on a soccer field for the first time. When I saw the inflatable movie screen, I was shocked to see something so big; the people on the screen appeared to be huge. I had never seen anything like that. The event was held for the public, outside the camp. A lot of people including me and my siblings arrived early to find a good spot to sit. We all gathered together on the floor to enjoy a movie. I was nine years old at the time, and I don't remember what kind of movie we were watching. But I vividly remember losing my siblings after the movie ended. As the people in the crowd stood up from the floor and began walking away, I looked up to find my siblings but encountered only unfamiliar faces everywhere. The crowd was dispersing quickly—moving in all directions even while the crowd noise remained in my ears. I cried as I searched for them through the tall crowd of strangers. I do not know why nobody in the crowd approached me to help me, I was sobbing heavily. I was a little boy who appeared to be in need of help.

It was getting dark and the sun was fading away. I felt hopeless, I didn't even bother to scream so they could hear my voice. I had tears in my eyes. Everyone was leaving the event quickly, but instead of standing there alone crying in fear, I followed a group of people walking in a direction I was not familiar with. I was crying as I continued to follow them. However, the group split up with two or three smaller groups taking different paths. I didn't know who to follow, so I hesitated a little bit before realizing that nobody was in my sight. I was standing alone and miles away from home. I needed to get home; my family was surely looking for me. I was thinking about how if I don't find my way home, my family could leave for the United States without me.

I walked feeling my sandals touching the dirt ground. I was passing a lot of tall trees, but not seeing clearly where I was or where I was going. I continued to walk in a hurry on the same trail. Ahead from a distance, all I saw was darkness; it felt like I was walking towards death. The sound of crickets didn't reduce the silent fear that kept my heart pounding. The night breeze caressing my body made me miss the warm feeling of being in the house with my family. I wanted to scream so my mother who was probably desperately looking for me could hear my voice. *"Mom, help me,"* I cried to myself. I was able to see things up close like the blades of grass on the side of the trail. Seeing where my feet stepped was not as challenging as seeing ahead in my direction; it terrified me to even look up and stare ahead. The darkness in front of me was so pitch black, I had to look down as I walked following my feet. I was afraid that somebody might lurk behind me and stab or kill me, so I was constantly looking back. On the left of the trail, I saw a cross made out of sticks planted on the ground. In a split second, I saw more crosses scattered all over my surroundings. I realized I was standing in a cemetery. There were no night lights and there were no buildings ahead. I was so alone and with no direction home.

I was scared and shaking at the same time. I started thinking about the mythical stories I used to hear at home about dead people coming to life. *Maybe Ayana is standing somewhere, but she can't possibly be here because we buried her in another camp. The wicked witches are probably flying right above me. God help, God help.* I turned around and ran away from that gloomy place. As I ran, a terrible fear fell over me. I felt like I was being chased by death. I felt a heavy sense of dread.

At last, I was found by two men who happened to be walking back to their homes in the middle of the night. I told them that I was from a refugee camp for United States immigrants. They took me with them and helped me find a place to sleep. I slept in a shanty house with a broken ceiling. It was raining all night, the rain would drop through the ceiling and cause my bed to get wet. The next morning, the two men walked me to the camp and released me to find my way home. When I arrived at my house, my mother was relieved to see me. But my life was filled with fear—the kind fears that followed me even as I grew

14

Dislocation and Relocation

My family was waiting to go to a land of possibilities. America was to us that place of possibilities. America seemed like heaven, and it existed beyond our imagination. But it wasn't just America. My family called countries like Australia or the United States with words that symbolized our dreams of escape from this life of struggles. America was a place of destiny. It was destined to be our new home. In our minds and, in reality, our future didn't exist in Tanzanian refugee camps or in Rwanda or in Burundi, we had to yearn for the American Dream.

In late 2007, Niyo had flown separately to the United States. Burundian immigrants chose voluntarily to come to the United States, but they did not choose where to settle within the country. Many were sent to Texas, Arizona, and

Minnesota, and, in some cases, families were separated during this process. Luckily for us, Niyo was sent to Vermont and we joined her there the next year.

On my last night in the camp, I barely slept, my eyes were open, and I couldn't stop thinking about being on an airplane for the first time. I used to stare at the sky with my hand over my forehead to see clearly in the bright sunlight as I watched airplanes flying by; they would fly high in the sky. They barely seemed to move as I kept my eyes on them. I followed an airplane with my eyes until it disappeared into the clouds. They were tiny as they flew through the clouds. They made noises that immediately directed everyone's attention to the sky. I would watch an airplane fly over our houses and think to myself, *another group of families is flying to Australia or the United States.* I did not know how large an airplane was up close; I had never seen one on the ground. But, from listening to what people were saying about planes, I learned that planes were bigger in actual size than they appeared high in the sky. I couldn't wait to see one.

It was November 2008, when we finally traveled to America. We first flew in a helicopter to Nairobi, the capital city of Kenya. When I boarded the plane with my family, we all knew we were going to a better place called the United States. We were not being forced to get on a boat, nor were we put in chains against our will. We were sitting in this luxurious airplane. We sat on comfortable seats where the back shoulders could lean into the soft cushions. These comfortable seats allowed us to relax. Then, we ate delicious food we had never tasted before. We had a TV screen in front of our seats. We watched a movie called *Shrek* --which seemed scary to me; I thought the green creature called Shrek was a living type of human and not an animation. When we lived in the camp, we lived without movie screens in front of us every day, so when I did see movies, I thought I was watching something that occurred in real-time.

We stopped over in Zürich, Switzerland. When we got off the airplane there, I confusedly thought it was our destination. It was night, and I saw the glittering lights of the western world. It was a beautiful place, the buildings were so tall they touched the sky. I couldn't see anything besides the smooth concrete floor that felt comfortable to walk on in my white sneakers. When we were inside the airport in Zürich, I kept looking around in amazement; it was like I was dreaming. They were people moving up and down on escalators. I looked up at the roof and couldn't believe how tall the building was. I felt small from the first floor. My eyes glanced at the escalator glass panel, the glass fencing panel on each floor, the glass doors, and the shining white walls. There were so many white people walking by. I was staring at them with fascination and wondering how different they are in comparison to me. I saw a fat white boy in a red winter jacket and denim pants walking in a space that looked like a big mall. He looked like the white people we watched on TV. We walked into what seemed to be a small room with an automatic sliding door. We stood in the little room, but I had no idea why until I felt a sudden movement, moving upwards and which gave me a fuzzy sensation. We were riding in an elevator for the first time.

We went back on another plane and continued to our destination. We resumed our routine which was watching *Shrek* and eating good food. I was exhausted. I had no idea when the plane landed or when we left; we were still in the airplane eating and falling asleep from boredom when we arrived in Burlington, Vermont. When we got off the plane, the ground had this white stuff that felt cold when you touched it. This white stuff was called snow and was like coldly frosted powder. The beautiful white snow made this new place look like heaven. It was a shining land that took place in our fantasy, but there we were standing in it.

The hardest adjustment for us was the cold that affected our bodies for the first time. We had to wear appropriate clothing for the cold. We were standing outside in front of the building at the airport with our luggage, waiting for somebody to pick us up in a car. We were feeling the cold for a minute until somebody handed us jackets. I had never worn a winter jacket before, but for the first time, I had to protect my body from the cold.

We got into a van and somebody drove us to our new house in Burlington. I kept looking out of the window. Desta, who was sitting next to me, was not pleased with the city or with the buildings. They were not what he expected. "There are no tall buildings like New York, " he said while closely examining the city.

The van pulled into the parking lot in front of our apartment. The driver said something in English I couldn't understand. Desta, who understood a little English, did his best to translate it. He pointed at the apartment and said in

Kirundi *"Iyi ni inzu yacu"* ("This is our house"). I saw Niyo standing outside the apartment waiting to meet us. At first, I couldn't recognize her. She was wearing tight jeans and a yellow puffer jacket. She looked different from the last I saw her. Her gorgeous cheeks were chubbier. Her arms and hips looked bountiful and full. We rushed out of the van not to see our new apartment, but to see our sister. We hugged her. Niyo had been living with a Burundian family as she waited for us to arrive. She eventually moved in with us and we all reconciled.

The landlord and our translator arrived instantly to show us the apartment. The translator was a man with a handsome smile who was also a Burundian refugee. Our new home was an apartment on one floor of a house. The house was painted white with overlapping wooden planks cladding the wall. There were porch stairs in front of the door. There was a bike locked on the stairs. It was an average size blue bike that looked brand new. It belonged to the neighbor who shared the apartment.

When we entered the apartment, I was amazed by how clean it was, the white walls were pure, the floor was as clean as anything I had ever seen. There was a big couch in the living room that I felt like I could sit on forever; I sat on it and started bouncing on it for a little bit.

Hoza looked thrilled with a smile on her face, touching everything in the house. All my siblings were amazed by the house, walking around the bedroom and kitchen like they were walking into a museum. My mother was in the kitchen touching the oven and trying to figure out how to use it. I looked around the house knowing that we made it, we were in America.

After we finally settled in, we sat inside all day; most of us were bored, especially me who loved the outdoors. I was not accustomed to wearing a jacket every time I stepped outside. So I accidentally walked outside in the snow wearing shorts, a sweater, and sandals. I was freezing down through my legs and toes. I saw white people walking by staring at me without words. The people in our neighborhood were never outside, we didn't even know who they were.

The street was mostly empty, with snow falling on top of every car that was parked in the street and making the street look white. I would often wonder if there were kids my age who lived next door, but I couldn't figure out if they lived in those houses that looked vacant and lifeless.

15

Fish Out Of Water

Everything felt different in this new place, except going back to school. I didn't want to be troubled by my past, but other children continued to haunt my present. The images of children teasing me, calling me names, and poking fun at me played and preyed in my mind. These ghastly images almost brought me to tears. I was sitting on the couch watching TV, and my mother came to me and said, "You are going to school tomorrow." My mood immediately dropped. I was not expecting to go to school. Being at home all day and enjoying TV was enough to keep me happy. I couldn't imagine the shyness I would feel while surrounded by strangers.

On my first day at school in America, I woke up in the morning feeling tired. I had an angry expression on my face as I got up to take shower. I tried to resist going by returning to sleep, but I was reminded of the day in the camp when Ife had to forcefully drag me to school.

As I prepared to go to school, I wore a long-sleeve white shirt that was worn by all refugees, including black denim pants with a match-ing jacket, and a blue winter jacket over it. There was a notebook and a pencil in my backpack. I put the backpack on my shoulder and walked to the bus stop sign in front of the house next door. It was cold, I could still feel  it through my jacket. There was a slush of snow on the ground, making it difficult to walk. The small white sneakers I was wearing struggled to walk through the heavy snow. I saw an Asian boy, who looked tall and lean with brown skin. He was coming out of the apartment next door with a back-pack. It was a large brick apartment with a fence around the back door. There was a sun porch in the front of the house facing the street. The boy was also walking to the bus stop in my direction. I didn't say anything to him; I stood next to him waiting for the bus to arrive. My lips were dry again, as usual when I was nervous.

I began my first day at Edmunds Middle School on January 12, 2009. When I saw the Edmunds Middle School building from the window of the bus I was amazed at how big it was. They were two gray brick buildings next to each with similar structures connected by an enclosed walkway. The building on the left and up on the hill of Main Street near Champlain College was Edmunds Elementary School. The building slightly down the hill on the right was Edmunds Middle School.

It was still freezing when all the students got off the bus. I followed them while feeling out of place. I walked inside the building, stood in the big hallway on the first floor, and looked around wide-eyed. I was astonished by two columns in the hall that looked like a nave arcade. I was feeling shy and anxious. I saw a huge crowd of white students walking through the hallway and opening their green and blue combination lockers. Their smiles looked so friendly; the students stared at me with such friendly smiles and that only made me feel more nervous. I was not used to seeing people so friendly. Especially because they were white people, I didn't know if it was a genuine smile. I only met two black kids, and unlike being with the white children, I felt comfortable in their presence. When I first made eye contact with this black boy, he stared at me and nodded his head as though he knew me.

Walking around the school was like being on stage for the first time while people watched me with scrutiny. I felt self-conscious; I barely moved my lips to speak. It was fear caused by social anxiety. It kept me from muting the cacophony of eyes of scrutiny and from quieting the thoughts that held my body into stillness.

Some days I would sit in a classroom with my hands held together on my thighs. My body was unsettled, shaking. During the passing hours, I would grow timid. I felt the warm dripping sweat through my armpit and thighs. I tried to never utter a word besides "yeah" while nodding my head.

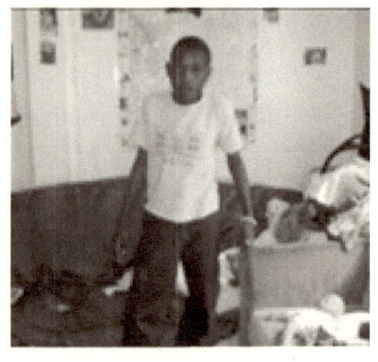

This feeling of shyness became so persistent that teachers and students found it a cause for concern. While sitting quietly in my English-as-a-Second Language (ESL) class, I felt strong feelings when I saw my ESL teacher's face. He had been trying to boost my mood. Sometimes he would say something funny to get a laugh or smile out of me. Even my classmate would join in to get rid of the sad look that seemed to remain on my face. When the teacher looked at me with a concerned face that suggested he had enough, I knew he saw something in me that was wrong. He thought I was frowning at everyone in class, like I didn't want to be there. But I did want to be there. *What am I supposed to do?* I thought. I was terrified to speak, I had a voice in my head threatening me if I dare to even stretch my arms. I couldn't lick my dry lips. My lips looked like they were stuck together and I felt as though a gun pointed at me if I spoke.

The problem was not be-
cause I couldn't speak the
language, all teachers knew
I understood English. The
moment I started school, my
teachers had made me watch
English learning tutorials on

the computer. It didn't take me long to learn English. The
words that felt foreign to me entered my mind quickly. The
black TV that my father had picked up on the street from
free stuff in our living room helped; every day after school,
I would sit on the living room couch and watch cartoons
shows on PBS kids. I loved shows like *Wordgirl* and *Curious
George*.

One of our close neighbors was a Burundian family we
had known from the refugee camp. They had arrived in Vermont before us, and they had helped us move in. They often
brought their four-year-old son over to our apartment for
babysitting. His name was Abel. On the weekend, we would
watch TV together on the couch. Abel loved to watch *Curious
George*, and he would cry every time I changed the channel. I
would speak to him in English because he barely understood
Kirundi. Abel had been born in Tanzania, but he was a baby
when his family came to the United States.

Mr. Reynolds, my ESL teacher, was a tall white man about
6'2" tall who kept trying to make me smile. I thought he was
too nice. It was clear to me that he was less frightening than
the teachers in the camp. I sat in the classroom, my eyes con-
centrated on the board while listening to every word he was

saying. Mr. Reynolds sounded like he was speaking quickly, and I couldn't pick up every word he said. He hated it when I nodded my head in response to a question, he wanted to hear me enunciate the word "yes" because I was often too quiet. My voice often cracked every time I tried to say something, I thought it was perhaps from having been silent for a long time.

The biggest problem was adjusting to the new culture. The food in the cafeteria couldn't go down on my stomach. I couldn't get close to the macaroni cheese, it smelled bad and caused my stomach to feel nauseated. My time in school was like being on stage for six hours. My hands were locked in my pocket as I walked. Sometimes I couldn't stretch my arms and feel relaxed like other students. The white students made me very uncomfortable. There was a particular white boy who was very nice to me. He sat next to me in social studies class. He had black hair and wore glasses. During class, he kept talking to me in such a way that I felt degraded; asking me things I already knew and helping me even though I didn't need help. People were very kind, but they didn't allow me to feel like everyone else, I felt too special. I would walk to class nervous and avoid eye contact. I would nod my head and pretend even though I was not used to people being so nice to me. I expected somebody to insult me, to call me names, and to humiliate me to a point where I have to shed a tear. There was another student who kept pronouncing my name wrong. My name was Furaha, but the boy kept calling me "Furar" with an r at the end. I was frustrated with him, so I often ignored him and allowed it. I remain shy and unwilling to speak. My relationship with other students was still not allowing me to express myself. It was really hard to smile; I had never been asked to smile until now. It was as though I was being asked to mask my emotion. I felt like being happy was not something I could switch off and on.

My parents received a phone call from the school to understand if anything was happening at home which was causing me to look sad and depressed. My mother was holding the landline phone in the kitchen, talking to the interpreter, and she saw me from the kitchen coming downstairs in the living room. The way she looked at me while holding the phone close to her ears was enough to indicate she was talking about me. I listened closely to what she was saying on the phone. "He is always talking at home, he is not sad" I heard her saying, "He just has social anxiety that vanishes when he is in a comfortable environment." I pumped my fist in agreement with her response and ran back upstairs in excitement. What my mother said was not far from the truth.

16

Adjusting to My New Life

Each day I was in school, I would feel like my body was being consumed with the presence of students. The students were like frightful bodies that made me feel alone. It was not until I decided to avoid their gaze that I learned how harmless they were. I was walking up the stairs to my class, looking down as I took steady steps. Suddenly I heard a voice of a student walking down the stairs as he passed by me. I did not see his face, all I heard was, "Hi Furaha". I felt the glow of his spoken words rise to my cheek. I was glad, but my eyes were still on the ground as I replied, "Hi" in a shaky voice.

After this interaction, I came to a realization that people loved to greet each other. Thus, I decided to keep my head up in anticipation of a greeting. Now I would see the faces of people who were greeting me. As I stroll back and forth to class wearing my backpack, I would try to relax my trembling hand. When a student said "hi" to me, I felt a joyful sensation in my body. It was like being seen. These students who came across to me saying "Hi" were male and female, but they were white students who knew me from class. I thought their smiles were filled with their kindness.

There was a problem though. The more I started running into students, the more I would find myself in situations where I had to speak. Students who recognized me would look to greet me and ask me how I was doing. The common greetings were "Hi" to "Hey."

I was still learning English, still in an ESL class with other students from different countries. Most of them were from Nepal and Thailand, and I was the only black person in the class. The lean Asian boy I saw leaving from the house next door was also in my class. He told me that his name was Dinesh. He was from Nepal and spoke Napali with classmates who were from Nepal. Dinesh had a lighthearted personality that also manifested through his thin and friendly face. I still remember his bright eyes and small lips. I thought he was a smart boy. He knew more English than I knew; after all, he had been living in the United States for two years. I carefully watched him writing in his notebook what seemed to be an entire paragraph in English. I couldn't even write long sentences yet. I envied him. I could tell he had an inclination to learn as I watched him attentively holding the pencil with his mind lost in the prose of English. Everyone else in the ESL class loved to be chatty except him.

Dinesh was good to me. He would try to cheer me up because I looked so shy. I could tell he wanted to be friends with me. Sometimes he would sit with me in the cafeteria for lunch. He did most of the talking. I just sat there listening and nodding my head. And yet, for some reason I didn't want to be closer to him. I wasn't comfortable having a friend at the moment. I was nervous and shy and wanted to be alone. I felt he might potentially touch me if we got too close and I didn't want to be touched yet. Perhaps I was remembering the pain I felt when I left Rugamba.

I knew one black student from the same country as me. He was the only person I could speak to in a complete sentence or in a language I was familiar with. He was in my home-room class which was my first class of the day. Every day we would pledge allegiance to the American flag. At first, I didn't know what to do. I saw everyone standing up, putting their hands on their chests while facing the flag in the corner of the room to our right, and repeating lines word for word. I got up and looked around in bewilderment while trying to speak along with everyone. I couldn't follow the lines; I was just mumbling until we got to the last sentence which was "justice for all." The Burundian boy's name was Orwin, and he sat further away from me with his classmates. He seemed socially integrated with other white students. He would speak with them, but I couldn't get close enough to hear what they were saying. So I was usually sitting alone between two empty seats and unbothered. In a silent manner, I was reduced to observing other students in the classroom who were talking among themselves.

Orwin had previously told me that he had also lived in the camp but had been living in Vermont for a while. He was in advanced ESL class, and he was already proficient in English. On my first day in school, he was my translator.

I recall meeting him for the first time. I arrived for check-in at the office on the right from the main entrance across from the principal's and nurse's offices. Orwin was called up at the office to translate for me since I didn't understand a word of English. He was wearing big baggy jeans that went over his shoes and a green hoodie. I could tell he spoke my language from looking at him; he looked like someone I knew from the camp. When I first made eye contact with him, he stared at me and nodded his head as if he knew me. Our hearts connected through the language we spoke. I felt that consciousness when we shared our beautiful laughter that fulfilled our existence. It was his kind laughter that helped define my confidence in school. Watching him in the hallway talking to white students with such worldly wit gave me hope that one day I will be able to do the same.

I hated the gym class, probably because I was not physically active. I was so skinny and weak I couldn't even pick up the basketball. We were in the gym shooting baskets for fun. I was struggling to get the ball into the basket. Because everyone had a ball, balls were bouncing everywhere on the court, making it hard to shoot, and suddenly out of nowhere a ball accidentally landed on my back shoulder with such a strong force, causing me to fall on the floor. For a second as I lay on the ground in pain, I thought somebody intentionally threw the ball on me, I had tears in my eyes. But as I tried to get myself up, a black boy touched me on the shoulder and said "I am sorry" and grabbed my hand to lift me from the floor.

From that moment, I knew those good people who were all around me.

At the end of the gym class, we all rushed into the locker room to change. I arrived in the locker room with other students, most of them were white with only three black students. I didn't bother talking to any students even though they would say "hi" to me occasionally, but nothing that seemed to lead to a conversation. Changing in front of them made me uncomfortable, so I started leaning towards the shower place with a curtain. I went in and changed into my denim pants and a white long-sleeve shirt.

My next class was the last for the day. The class felt like an eternity. My mind was racing with the clock. I stared at the clock like a starving man waiting for food. The clock hung on the wall as I waited for the minute hand to complete its hour and reach 3 o'clock. When it tilted to 3 PM, my mind predicted the bell that allowed all the students to storm out of their classes and fill up the hallways. The moment of relief was achieved. When school was over, I finally breathed the beautiful air on Monday afternoon.

I walked to the bus stop with the other students. Like always, I was used to sitting alone on the bus. I do not know why nobody sat next to me; maybe it was because nobody knew me. On this day, a girl who I thought was passing by me unexpectedly paused for a second before sitting next to me.

On this awkward day, somebody made my life a little more interesting. I thought this day was so different it felt like a dream. I do not remember the clothes she wore, but she was an Asian girl with black hair, thin lips, and small eyelashes. The girl looked at me with a smile that shocked my nerves. I wanted to smile back, but I was so shy I kept shaking as I stared at her polite smile. She offered me a chocolate candy that was rounded and wrapped-in-foil. I automatically began having deja vu. I pictured the moment when I reached out my hand to receive the candy. The time stopped and I was no longer moving in motion. I reached out my hand and received the candy. I was reminded of a movie I recently watched in ESL class called *Bridge to Terabithia.* I felt like I had met this girl before:

> *The sun drops at the shining and flourishing flowers.*
> *Nature calls for the days when we are young.*
> *Living in our imagination, holding hands and gazing at the magical world,*
> *There is a love of being young.*
> *This is our kingdom,*
> *You can hear the wind blowing the trees as we run around laughing in joy*
> *We are free from the troubled hours, we are young and in love.*

I went home on the bus sitting next to the girl with a beautiful sunny day shining into the window. She gave me butterflies in my heart. I had never felt so hot and nervous on the bus home. I could feel my heart beating fast. I was shaking while holding the candy in my right hand. My left hand resting on my thigh had not moved an inch. I felt frozen in one position, I couldn't make eye contact with her until she reached out her hand to press the bus stop button to indicate her destination. Her stop was not far from my house. She got up from her seat and said goodbye. After she left, I finally felt relaxed, I took my hand off my thigh and stretched my neck. I arrived home thinking about her. I also kept thinking about the movie in class, I thought, together, our young imaginations stared at my beautiful soul. I kept wishing we walked together to the edge of the Green Mountains to stare at the beautiful landscape of Vermont, but it was still nothing but a fantasy.

The next school day, I was in the cafeteria for lunch, sitting alone at one of the tables. The busy cafeteria noise proceeded to land in my ears, making it hard to gather my thoughts. The mashed potatoes on my tray tasted good, but after only three bites, I was already done. I drank the carton of milk and my stomach felt fully nourished. I didn't eat much, but looking at my skinny body, you might think I needed to eat more. I looked up around the cafeteria table and spotted two white boys who were in my homeroom class. They were twins, identical with blond hair, tall and slim bodies. They were sitting with other white students including two girls. One of the twins turned his head in my direction and met my gaze. Then I tried to look away in embarrassment, but he started gesturing at his hand to call me. I read his gesture and walked to his table with my tray. I sat down with his group of friends. Everyone on the table had a smile on their face as they stared at my timid face. I didn't recognize any of them except the twins who somehow knew my name.

"Hi, Furaha. how are you?" One of the twins said while looking at me with a smile.

"I am good," I said in a shaking voice.

"Good," he said with a face of gladness.

I remained silent while looking down at the mashed potatoes I couldn't eat. I felt ashamed for not knowing their names. I was bad with names. So many white students had told me their names, but those names would slip out of my mind quickly from the moment I met another person who had blond hair or black hair.

Meanwhile at home, the fear of gaining weight was on my mind. Hoza and Fana were slowly changing their appearance, getting chubby cheeks and hips. I was starting to look heavy myself. I would wrap my hand around my wrist to measure the size of it. This time my wrist felt bigger, I felt like my hand couldn't wrap around it. Access to food was not difficult as it had been in the camp, particularly fast food and sweets. There was a box of donuts on the dinner table in the kitchen. The refrigerator had soda, orange juice, milk, a bowl of rice, and beans. We ate anytime, we didn't have to wait for our mother to cook food. We sat on the living couch, eating all day while watching TV. Nobody went a day feeling hungry. A white lady from a protestant church in South Burlington which we all attended every Sunday brought us food every other week.

The church van that came to pick us up every Sunday morning. I recall I would get irritated when my mother woke us up to get ready for church. I didn't like waking up at 10:00 am on Sunday, especially because I would stay up late on Saturday night watching Spongebob. The next morning, I would feel so sleepy, I would desire to sleep in.

The church was bigger in comparison to our Anglican church in the Tanzanian camp. It was at the time called Community Bible Church. Looking from a distance, on the side of the Williston Road, the church looked like two flat buildings with gable roofs facing the road with a connected veranda entrance.  The larger building on the left had a black cross attached to the wall of the gable.

The people at the church loved us. The pastor was a middle-aged, balding white man who wore small metal flame glasses. He always had a smile on his face. He preached with this incredible wisdom that touched our soul. There was a middle-aged white lady who loved to give us hugs and kisses on the forehead every time she saw us at the church. At the time, we felt that the kiss on the forehead was a culture shock. In the camp, we didn't express each other with such closeness. Thus when the woman approached me with excitement and love on her face and kissed my forehead, I always felt uncomfortable.

Desta and I knew that gaining weight was inevitable; the food was delicious but as new Americans, we didn't want to look like the fat people on TV. We had been planning to avoid eating too much, so we would practice fasting. But when our hunger was too much, we would eat just rice for the entire day. As I looked at myself in the mirror I knew I was losing weight. I noticed a reduction in my body; my shoulders were lean, my chest was flat, my cheeks were sunken in, and my arms looked like bones.

I loved to wear a long sleeve white shirt with a photo of a hockey player on the front. Including long and wide black pants that didn't fit me. I looked underweight, but I was not concerned, in fact, I loved it. Abel's father came home one afternoon and saw me sitting on the couch. As he took his right hand to firmly greet me, he asked my mother, who was 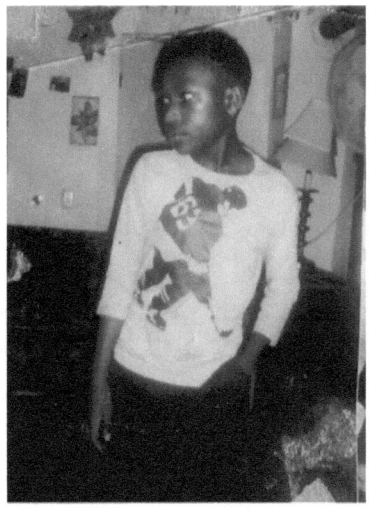 also standing in the living room, if they fed me enough food. I looked embarrassed as I watched my mother trying to respond, "I don't know, he has never been someone who eats a lot," she said.

During class, everyone was talking about how we only had two weeks left before the summer break. It was almost the end of the school year. It was a beautiful day, the sun was shining out of the glass window. Some students were too distracted looking outside. For a state where it is cold and snowing for most of the school year, the days of spring felt like heaven's doors.

Luckily since we were close to the end of the year, all students stepped outside for yearbook photos. We gathered around holding hands to make an EMS sign which stood for Edmunds Middle school. I remember I was nervous because I was holding a girl's hand. She was a white girl with black hair wearing denim shorts and a white sleeveless shirt. Our hands held together for a long time, I could feel the sweat between our hands. My heart was beating every second, I had not said a word to her. I was locked in my shyness.

We were supposed to keep holding hands with the same person throughout as we shifted into different activities. While I was still holding her hand, my homeroom teacher approached me and asked if I could speak French. "Do you speak French" he asked. I looked at him while trying to figure out where he had gotten that idea. I had a French name back in the camp, but here in the US, everyone called me "Furaha" which is not a French name. It's Swahili. *Is this because of my accent, or is he confusing me to another black kid who speaks French*, I wondered as I replied, "No, I don't speak French." I used to study French when I lived in the camp, but our education was cut short.

I had not said a word to the girl throughout this time. As my hand was finally parting from her, I looked her in the eyes while nervously letting go of her hand. For some reason, I didn't want to let go of her hand. She slowly walked away from me with her face looking back at me. The image of her face stayed in my mind, it followed on my way home.

When I arrived home, Hoza, who was in 5th-grade at Edmunds Elementary School, was already home; she was sitting on the living room couch watching the Disney channel. Ajani, Desta, and Fana were still in high school. Ife was working at the Hilton hotel as a laundry attendant. Niyo was also working at the Hilton, but in housekeeping. My mother was still yet to return from work; she also worked in housekeeping service at a different hotel in South Burlington. My father was sitting in the kitchen listening to Rwandan gospel music. Sometimes later in the afternoon, I would come home from the Boys & Girls Club, and he would be playing some gospel music called by the Rwandan gospel group, Rehoboth Ministries. One of my favorite songs from Rehoboth Ministries was *Bakundwa*. Everytime it played on the living room TV, I would feel the joy of being at home.

> *Mbonye yuko imibabaro*
> *y'iki gihe ntagereranya*
> *nu ubwiza byo mwijuru.*
> *bakundwa turi abana b'Imana*
> *Kuko tuzamara ni byo byerekana*
> *ariko, ibizi neza*
> *igihe Yesu yerekanye*
> *tuzasa na we*
> *Benedata, mureke gucika intege*
> *Uwo twategereje hafi kuza*

Muri iyi si hariho ibibazo n'ibigeragezo

ariko, hahirwa umuntu ubyhaganira

Kuko, namakunasha azahabwa

ikamba ryasezeranijwe ry'ubuzima bw'iteka

I see that the suffering of this time

Does not compare to the beauty of heaven.

Beloved we are God's children.

our reflection is not yet known

however, what we know well

When Jesus is revealed,

We will appear like him.

Brethren, do not give up.

The one we have been waiting for is near to come.

There are troubles and trials in this world,

But blessed is the one who preserve them.

After overcoming, everyone will given

A promised crown of eternal life.

As a family, we sat peacefully in the living room watching TV. This time Desta and Ife were present. Ife had the TV remote in his hand; he was sitting on the couch with Desta. My father was also sitting on the couch with Niyo. I was sitting down below them on the carpet with Hoza. Ajani and Fana were in the kitchen helping my mother prepare food. They were cooking rice, chicken, and Cassava leaves. We were watching a family comedy movie called *Daddy Day Camp*. We were laughing together like a family. My father got off the couch, walked into the kitchen to use his sewing machine. He turned on his radio and played one of his favorite songs. I smiled because I could hear my mom, Fana, and Ajani from the kitchen singing. *"Mwami kubaho ntagufite/Binter' ubwoba n' amaganya."* Our apartment was full of life.

Ife handed the remote to Desta, and he tiredly moved up from the couch while stretching his arms.. He said he was going to work. I stood up on the floor to take his seat. I curiously looked at Desta. He was firmly holding

the remote in his hand. As I watched him looking at the TV screen, his gentle eyes and calm look on his face reminded me of something. I had never known him, he had been a stranger until now.

In this post-colonial society, we had to find meaning in our new world. The songs we sang were here to keep our spirits alive.